A
Pond View
Biography

Born at Barnoldswick (then in Yorkshire, now in Lancashire), Ken Wilson qualified in architecture and town planning and became Deputy Borough Architect of the London Borough of Bromley. During his service with Bromley he designed the Churchill Theatre and Central Library complex.

Now living at Shoreham, Kent, he is fulfilling his ambition to work full-time as an artist, writer and public speaker. His paintings have often been exhibited in London and the North of England – and this is the fifteenth book he has had published.

Everybody's heard of BLONDIN

written and illustrated by

Ken Wilson

POND VIEW BOOKS

© Hawthorns Publications Limited 1990
Reprinted 1997

Published by
Hawthorns Publications Limited,
Pond View House,
6A High Street,
Otford,
Sevenoaks,
Kent. TN14 5PQ

ISBN 1 871044 35 9

Printed by Longmore Press Ltd, Otford, Sevenoaks, Kent, TN14 5PG

PREFACE

When I was very young, my father told me that Blondin had walked over Niagara Falls on a tightrope. I could not understand how the rope had been fixed and this unanswered question remained in my mind for nearly sixty years.

On returning to the subject, I could find only one book on Blondin, written in the early 1860s, and it did not provide the information. None of my other enquiries supplied the answer, so I was drawn into further research on the man and his remarkable feats. This work took me to France, where he was born; to the United States and Canada, where he is still regarded as the greatest of the Niagara stunters; and finally back to England where he appeared at many entertainment centres including the Crystal Palace and Alexandra Park.

This book is the product of that research. As far as I am aware, it is Blondin's only biography, a story which surely deserves to be told. I have been able to establish relatively little about his private life: contemporary interviewers received only accounts of his triumphs, nothing about the man himself.

Blondin's reticence seems to have been transmitted to his family. When his last surviving daughter was interviewed, late in her life, she talked only of the time when, at the age of five, her father had pushed her in a wheelbarrow across a rope high up in the Crystal Palace.

Without doubt, Blondin was a great artiste and a superlative showman. It is for his performances that he is remembered and it is because of his amazing feats that everybody (or virtually everybody!) has heard of Blondin.

November 1989   Ken Wilson

In the spring of 1858, a visitor to Niagara was seeing the Falls for the first time. Like so many others, before and since, he marvelled at the great natural spectacle but, in his imagination, he saw something else — a new bridge. Not a bridge of steel or concrete but of rope; a single strand of rope, measuring no more than three or four inches in diameter, and he the only person using it. The visitor's name was Jean François Gravelet, known as Blondin. It would not be long before the world knew that nickname.

He returned to Niagara the following year. Since his previous visit, Blondin had been secretly formulating a plan. This was his methodical way of working: everything considered in advance, down to the last item of detail. Risks were carefully assessed and special techniques devised to minimise them; equipment was given meticulous consideration. It was the professional approach and, at thirty five, he had been a professional for nearly thirty years. The folly of not using the correct equipment had been painfully demonstrated to him at the age of five and a half years.

3

During that year of 1829, a troupe of travelling entertainers arrived in the small French town of Hesdin in the Pas de Calais, close by the battlefield of Agincourt. They pitched their tents near the home of André Gravelet, his wife Eulalie and their small son Jean François. The boy, with others nearby, spent hours at the camp site watching acrobats, tumblers and other performers at their daily practice. Jean François had eyes mainly for the funambulist — tightrope walker — and he was amazed and fascinated as the young man in blue smock, spangles and fleshings rehearsed 'Amazing Feats On The Hempen Line'. He could not wait to try for himself some of the tricks he had seen and, while his parents were out, he tied a clothes line to the backs of two chairs placed a short distance apart. He borrowed his father's fishing rod as a balancing pole then he, who would one day be the world's most famous funambulist, made his first attempt and sharply learned the folly of using inadequate equipment. It was a lesson he never forgot.

If such things are hereditary, it was André Gravelet who passed down to his son the aptitude for balancing. He, too, had been a tightrope walker and dancer. He described himself as such when registering the birth of Jean François on 28 February 1824. The following day, André, with two friends as witnesses, went to the Office of the Provost, Mayor and Public Officer of Hesdin to present him with a baby boy, as the register duly recorded. André signed the entry, as did the first witness Joseph Plancart who, at twenty five years of age already owned his own inn, but the second, Gaspard Hancart, a befuddled bartender of seventy four, hesitated and then declared he was unable to sign. It was assumed — wrongly — that he could not write and he was asked to make his mark. Then the Mayor read out the particulars that had been set down and again asked him to witness them. Still he would not do so. What was going on in old Gaspard's mind was not explained; for whatever reason he refused to perform the small service required by law to which, presumably, he had previously given his agreement. Despite the legal requirement, the Mayor waived the formality.

It had been some time since André Gravelet had walked a tightrope, or danced, or had worked at all. At thirty four, he was a sick man. Most of his adult life had been spent in Napoleon Bonaparte's Grande Armée. Through years of campaigning in Europe his health was undermined. After surviving Austerlitz, Wagram and the disastrous retreat from Moscow, he rejoined the veterans, after the Emperor's escape from Elba, and followed him to Waterloo.

Eulalie Gravelet (*née* Merlet) waited a long time for her soldier to return and she was thirty when their son was born.

Like so many of his generation, who knew little else but army life, André found it difficult to settle down. It tended to be past glories and not present practicalities that occupied his thoughts.

Jean François was not deterred by the failure of his first attempt on the rope. Characteristically, he reassessed the situation. He turned for assistance to a family friend who lived nearby. Jacques Le Brun was a veteran of the Imperial Navy, having served on a French man o' war. He too spent much of his time telling stories of 'the good old days' and he was not really considered by the Gravelets to be ideal company for their son, but there is often a bond between the old and the young and these two spent a lot of time together. Jacques had already taught the boy to climb trees and other obstacles with the agility of an ocean-going crewman; now he supplied some ship's cable, of more than adequate strength, and a length of wooden spar for use as a balancing pole. In secret they met in the woods, at some distance from the houses. The rope was slung between two trees at a safe but soon increasing height and, with the unflagging encouragement of his nautical mentor and a grim determination ahead of his years, Jean François' first uncertain steps became more confident and progressively assured.

5

When their son's proven skill and undoubted virtuosity was announced to the parents by Le Brun, and ably demonstrated by the boy at the secret hideaway in the woods, André and Eulalie were delighted. It was then and there decided that Jean François should have the very best training available. This was to be found in the ancient city of Lyons and the family travelled there at the earliest opportunity.

Lyons was the third largest city in France and capital of the Department of Rhône. It lies at the confluence of the Rhône and Saône rivers, in the shade of the Fourvière Hill. It was this defensive and commercial setting that attracted the Romans to build a fortified town there. The magnificent theatre indicates its cultural status.

It became the centre of the silk industry which had recently been revolutionised by the invention of the Jacquard loom. The old town was dominated by the twelfth century Gothic cathedral of St Jean.

6

The famous École de Gymnase, acknowledged to be the finest centre for the training of acrobats, brought the Gravelets to Lyons. Its. Principal had earned this reputation by the introduction of radical new methods. L'École now used only gentle persuasion, demonstration and encouragement by which to achieve its professional standards.

Historically it had been assumed that only fear would induce performers to undertake progressively more dangerous acts for the entertainment of an audience. Most of the pupils were taken from the workhouse, theoretically as apprentices. If some died in the course of their training it was accepted as an inevitable cost in the dangerous profession for which they were being prepared. Instructors used brutality to command instant obedience. The most notorious was Ducrow, who subsequently became one of France's leading gymnastic performers. He was reputed never to have used a single word of encouragement and perpetually carried a heavy cane with which to beat pupils remorselessly, whether they warranted punishment or not.

Jean François was enrolled as a residential pupil and such was his progress, under the benevolent tutelage, that he made his first professional appearance within six months, billed as 'The Little Wonder'. He had not reached his sixth birthday.

Two years later he appeared by royal command before the King of Sardinia in Turin.

There was nothing unique about doing something 'unique'. Rope-walkers had been performing the impossible for centuries. There are many reports of such in the histories of ancient Egypt and classical Greece. They formed a prominent part of the Roman circus. Emperor Caligula was an accomplished walker on the suspended rope and claimed enormous fees for his appearances. In Nero's time elephants were shown doing balancing acts on specially strengthened ropes; even carrying other elephants on their backs.

Down through the ages, the 'impossible' of one day became the commonplace of another. By the thirteenth century the Egyptians were again the acknowledged masters of the art and demonstrated their prowess throughout Europe and Asia. At Constantinople they slung lines between the masts of ships in the harbour on which to display their amazing skills.

Many lost their lives, not only by accident but also by execution, because they were thought to be in league with the Devil. A horse, which had been taught to do a number of tricks, was publicly tried in Lisbon in 1601 and, on being convicted of witchcraft, was burned at the stake.

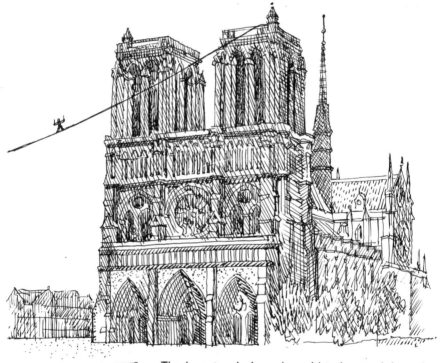

The 'spectacular' can be said to have originated in France when Isabel, Queen of Charles VI, arrived in Paris. A rope was tied from the highest house on the Pont St Michel to the top of one of the west towers of Notre Dame. Froissart walked down the rope with a lighted candle in each hand, singing as he went.

The English have never excelled in the art of rope-walking, although it has been popular as a spectator sport. In Tudor times the spire of old St Paul's was the scene of a number of spectaculars. Philip of Spain, husband of Mary I, witnessed 'a walk' performed by a Dutchman called Peter, who was paid £16.13s.4d. A Dutchwoman also performed the feat of walking down a rope stretched from the tip of the spire, just below the weathervane, to the ground in front of the Dean's house. Edward VI was treated to a special display by a man from Aragon, who slid down the rope head first with arms and legs outstretched. Pepys' diary records other events in Restoration times.

Marie Antoinette's court enjoyed the spectacle so much that the French attained superiority in the field and held on to it, until Blondin put his personal stamp on its history. Before him, Madame Saqui was the acknowledged leader, she having traversed La Place de la Concorde in her seventieth year.

It was events of this scale of 'uniqueness' which Blondin was determined to surpass.

Blondin was the first to use a horizontal tightrope. Earlier performers had used a sloping rope if it was pulled tight, or a slack one if it was slung between two points of equal height.

9

André Gravelet died at the age of forty three, in his son's ninth year. Twelve months later Eulalie also died, just before her fortieth birthday.

At ten years of age orphan Jean François was already capable of supporting himself financially. When his father was in the Grande Armée, his comrades coined a nickname for him because of his light coloured hair. They called him 'Blondin'. Jean François adopted it as a stage name and from then on 'The Little Wonder' became Blondin.

He was already receiving offers to appear in public, but he remained at the school until the kindly Principal advised him that he had advanced beyond the point where they could teach him anything further.

During the next eighteen years Blondin lived the circus life of the travelling entertainer and established such a wide reputation, for the skill and originality of his performance, that he received engagements all over the continent.

In 1851, at the age of twenty seven, while appearing in Paris, he was approached by the agent of the Ravel Family, the most famous acrobatic troupe in France. He joined them on a tour of America under a two-year contract with the great showman Phineas T. Barnum.

Barnum was born in Bethel, Connecticut in 1810. He began his career as a showman at the age of twenty five but had little success until nine years later when he exploited Charles Stratton as General Tom Thumb. Stratton was a midget, only two feet in height, although he later grew to forty inches tall (1 metre). Barnum made him world famous, exhibiting him twice in England, in 1844 and 1857. Subsequently, Stratton married Lavinia Warren, another midget, even shorter than himself. They lived happily together until his death in 1883 at the age of fifty five. Lavinia married another midget, Count Magri, an Italian, who took over the title of Tom Thumb. She died in 1919 and he, the year after.

It was another twenty years before Barnum formed 'The Greatest Show On Earth' with his partner Bailey. It was a monster combination of circus, menagerie and exhibition of human freaks. It made him an immense fortune.

Blondin sailed for New York in 1851. On the voyage an incident occurred which is best described in the heroic prose of a contemporary report:

'During the raging of a violent storm, a young man of noble birth, who chanced to be a passenger on board the same ship with him, was suddenly precipitated overboard as the ship rose and sunk in the black abyss of waves that yawned around her. Blondin, with a bound, sudden as that of the panther, leaped after him; the winds shrieked and howled like demons let loose, and the hissing, surging waves swept over them mercilessly; but the strong swimmer breasted them notwithstanding, and courageously approached the drowning man in time to save him. Struggling gallantly against desperate odds, he reached the ship and was drawn up in safety, but not before he had lashed his fainting companion on the rope that was thrown out to him.'

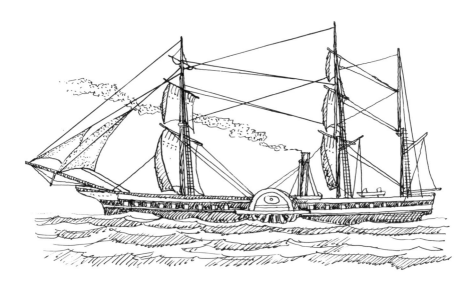

Blondin's rescue of the young man from the sea, an element in which he had no experience, is surprising; more so in view of his way of carefully assessing any problem before attempting the risk. This kind of bravery is rare, even among people who trade on a brand of courage in their own field.

Ducrow, the former instructor at L'École de Gymnase, in his prime as a performer, was regarded as the most daring horseback rider of his day. Many of his leaps over hurdles were considered to be virtually impossible, yet he achieved them without apparent effort. At the height of his fame he frequently visited Yorkshire as the guest of Mr Lascelles, later the Earl of Harewood, and joined the York and Ainsty Hunt. Where his host would charge over fences with both feet dropped from the stirrups, Ducrow would invariably hold back and usually find some lower and safer place to take the jump.

A more typical example of Blondin's method of working was demonstrated when he was appearing with the Ravels at Niblo's Gardens in New York. The star of the show was Antoine Ravel but Blondin's abilities were rapidly challenging this order of importance. The finale of Antoine's act was a sketch in which a prisoner, played by Antoine, escaped from a squad of soldiers by a backward leap over the tips of their fixed bayonets. One morning the act was being rehearsed on stage. While to the audience the leap was spectacular, there being about twenty men, by carefully placing the soldiers in relation to himself, Antoine only had to clear two bayonets and the space between them. It was a worked out stunt where the risks were minimised. It had brought applause on two continents.

Blondin appeared on stage as the men were being moved into their positions for the rehearsal. He was on his way out of the theatre and was dressed in his outdoor clothes. Without announcing his intention, he took three or four strides and threw a double somersault over the entire squad, lengthways, then proceeded out of the theatre without a word. It reduced the star's spectacular to absurdity.

There is no doubt that Blondin had been considering the act in its present form carefully and knew it was far below his own capabilities. He would have rehearsed it in secret, with accurately worked out dimensions, probably in the shoes and clothes he was wearing on the day. The act was never repeated; it confirmed the opinion, already held by many, that not only had he outstripped the Ravels but was on the brink of performing something unique.

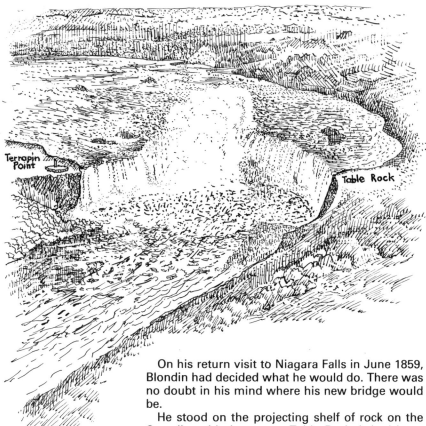

Terrapin
Point

Table Rock

On his return visit to Niagara Falls in June 1859,
Blondin had decided what he would do. There was
no doubt in his mind where his new bridge would
be.

He stood on the projecting shelf of rock on the
Canadian side known as Table Rock. It had been
reduced in size by a landslide nine years before,
taking with it a coach parked on it but not the horse,
tethered to a tree on the rock left behind. The driver
had jumped from the falling coach and landed
safely.

To Blondin's right, in a sweeping arc over 2,000
feet (606m) wide, the Horseshoe Falls plunged 174
feet (52.8m) into the turbulent white water below,
sending a cloud of spray three times as high into
the air. Through the spray he could see Terrapin
Point on the American bank.

To the left, separated from the Horseshoe by
Goat Island, were the American Falls, slightly
higher at 184 feet (55.7m) but narrower by half and
quite as awe inspiring.

Blondin's bridge of rope would stretch from
Terrapin Point to Table Rock.

The name Niagara comes from an Iroquois word meaning river or the strait. Early Jesuit missionaries attempted to write it as Onuiaahra and it appeared on maps as early as 1641.

When white men first entered the interior of America, the Iroquois Indian League was a well organised political entity, even though it numbered only about 17,000 people. For over 150 years, the Iroquois resisted all efforts to dislodge them from Niagara.

Their villages were fairly permanent settlements, usually occupied for about twenty years until the cornfields became infertile and supplies of firewood ran out. They lived in long houses, each occupied by up to thirty families.

Tribal matters were settled on a loosely democratic basis, and Onuiaahra, or Niagara, was cited as a model for the first constitution of the United States.

The first white men to record seeing the Falls were, like Blondin, also French. They were Father Hennepin and Lieutenant La Motte, who arrived there on the 6 December 1678, as part of an advance party, seeking an overland route from Quebec to the Gulf of Mexico. The priest made a sketch of the Falls which appeared in his book *New Discovery* in 1697. It was not a good likeness, although it was correct in basic detail. The height was grossly distorted and wrongly estimated at 600 feet (181.8m). It was also claimed that the noise could be heard forty five miles away.

At the beginning of the seventeenth century, when the French colonised the north bank of the river, the land was occupied by the Neutral Indians. They were on good terms with their neighbours, the Hurons and the Iroquois. In 1615 a French explorer, Samuel de Champlain, supplied the Hurons with guns for a raid on the Iroquois. This had far-reaching effects which led to the extermination of both the Huron and the Neutral nations in southern Ontario. It also marked the start of Indian opposition to the French and their collaboration with the British.

In 1812 America declared war on Britain and on the 25 July the most fierce action of the whole war took place on the Canadian side of Niagara Falls. It was the Battle of Lundy's Lane and it was fought at the junction of that Lane with the old Portage Road, which had been used for centuries to carry goods over land to bypass the Falls. Some 2,000 British, Canadian and Indian forces opposed about 5,000 Americans. The battle started about six o'clock in the evening and lasted till midnight. Casualties were heavy on both sides, but the action was indecisive. At the end of hostilities the township of Stamford was left in burning ruins.

A new town grew on the site and was re-named Drummondville, after Sir Gordon Drummond who commanded the British troops. By 1817 the population was 1,200 and three years later the tourists began to find their way to the area.

William Forsyth built the first hotel in 1822 and named it the Pavilion. His father had been granted 388 acres of land fronting the crest of the Horseshoe Falls. The hotel was constructed of timber in the colonial style and faced the Portage Road. Before the railways arrived, most travellers came on horseback or by coach. Forsyth began to run his own coaches. He built the first staircase down the bank of the gorge, near Table Rock, and ran the first ferry service across the lower river.

Competition soon developed. Other hotels were built and Forsyth lost his monopoly. He came into conflict with the military authorities who owned a strip of land along the river frontage, by fencing the land off for the use of his customers. Attempts to retain his advantageous position by costly litigation had the opposite effect and eventually forced him out of business in 1832.

Forsyth was the promoter of the first 'stunt' at Niagara Falls. With two other hotel proprietors, John Brown of the Ontario House and P. Whitney of the Eagle, he bought a condemned lake schooner named *Michigan.* They organised a publicity promotion announcing that the *Michigan Pirate* ship, with a cargo of ferocious animals, would pass through the rapids above the Horseshoe Falls and 'plunge down its grand precipice into the basin below'.

The event took place on 8 September 1827 at 3 o'clock in the afternoon. The 'cargo' consisted of two bears, a buffalo, two racoons, a dog and a goose. The 'pirate crew' were placed 'in effigy' around the deck. A crowd estimated at between 15,000 and 30,000 came to watch it happen. The schooner was towed out from Black Rock to Navy Island. This was well upstream and passengers could travel on this stage of the journey for half a dollar a head.

When all but the cargo had been taken off, it was released into the main stream. The two bears were not secured but all the other animals were either caged or tethered. As the boat entered the rapids above the Falls, both bears abandoned ship and succeeded in reaching the bank safely. The rest went over and perished.

Nobody seemed to protest at this cruelty. No official action was taken to stop it. From the hoteliers' points of view it had the desired effect of attracting visitors to Niagara Falls. More and more hotels were built. The Front, on the Canadian side which overlooked both Falls, began to develop as a 'golden mile' with sideshows, souvenir vendors, gamblers, hustlers and pimps and became a tourist centre.

Among the crowd watching the *Michigan*'s last voyage was a young mill worker from Pawtucket Falls, New England. His name was Sam Patch.

Two years later he was back again. He obtained permission from the Porter family, who owned Goat Island, to put up a wooden tower on their river bank. It was about 100 feet (30.3m) high and had a small platform on top. Two converging ladders gave both stability and access to the platform.

Unlike the hoteliers, Sam could not afford to run a publicity campaign, so only a tiny handful of people turned up, one chilly day in September 1829, when Sam Patch became Niagara's first human stunter by leaping 100 feet (30.3m) into the river below.

Sam Patch did get some publicity from his leap and he used it to some advantage to arrange an appearance at the City of Rochester, some eighty miles away on the southern shore of Lake Ontario. The Genessee River passes through there and descends to lake level through a series of three falls. The Upper Falls are the highest at about 98 feet (29.7m) and, for him, had the attraction of being close to the city centre.

Sam built a smaller tower which took his platform to a height of about 126 feet (38.2m) above the water level at the foot of the Falls. Learning from his previous errors, he got some money together and had some large posters painted. 'Higher yet!', they proclaimed. 'Sam's Last Leap!'

There were very large crowds at the Upper Falls at 2 o'clock on the chosen day in November 1830. It was a Friday. Friday the thirteenth. The posters turned out to be prophetic. It was Sam's last leap; they didn't find his body until the following spring.

It is unlikely that Blondin had ever heard of Sam Patch, or the *Michigan* incident. He would not have approved of either. These were mere stunts with no skill involved or professional expertise.

His own approach was motivated by commercial considerations, but primarily there was a challenge in attempting something no one else had tried before. He was an adventurer and to be called a stunter would have been offensive to him. But he was also a showman and would need publicity.

The *Niagara Falls Weekly Gazette* was owned by Mr Poole and Mr Sleeper. Only two weeks before Blondin's arrival, they had taken the decision to try and make it the *Niagara Falls Daily Gazette*. It was an enormous risk. They faced the problem of finding enough items of interest to fill the paper each day and the pattern had to be set from the first issue.

A few days before that first issue was due to appear, a short and somewhat undistinguished Frenchman arrived in their office and introduced himself as M. Blondin. He did not seem at the time to be the solution to their immediate problem. When he told them he intended to walk across Niagara Falls on a tightrope they first thought it was a hoax. When they realised he meant it, they told him he was mad. Then their journalistic experience took over and they got him a chair. Either way, it was copy, good copy ... excellent copy! After further discussion, Mr Poole and Mr Sleeper pledged the full support of the *Daily Gazette.* They had nothing to lose. If it was a hoax, it was sufficiently lunatic to sell newspapers. If he did it, their paper had been the first to back him. If he killed himself, they had been the first to tell him he was mad.

The next person to tell Blondin he was mad was Harry Colcord. The two first met in Boston in 1858. The contract with the Ravels and Barnum was due to expire the following May. Harry knew the American show business scene very well and Blondin asked him to be his agent.

After Blondin's first visit to Niagara Falls, Harry noticed that none of his suggestions, or offers of contracts to work elsewhere which he produced, seemed to arouse the slightest interest. It was obvious that his client had something else on his mind and when he heard, he reacted in exactly the same way as Mr Poole and Mr Sleeper. 'It's a joke!' he said: then, after seeing that Blondin wasn't amused, exclaimed, 'You're mad!'

Once he realised that the plan was definitely on, Harry concentrated on the promotion.

This was premature. There were a number of problems to be overcome. The first was the rope itself. To span the gorge it had to be 1,300 feet long (393m) and, to be strong enough, the diameter would have to be 3¼ inches (82mm). A rope this size could not be manufactured in one length and would have to be spliced. For stability guy lines of lighter rope would be required, at regular intervals, passing through clips and weights on the rope and secured to pegs or trees on the bank.

The length of line would probably be about 2,600 feet (788.7m). When the cost was worked out by the ropemakers Fassett and Saehlenou, it amounted to 1,300 dollars.

Blondin did not possess that amount of money.

Financial backing was needed, and before parting with their cash, sponsors had to know that the event was positively feasible. The *Daily Gazette* had pledged their support so long as it didn't cost them anything. Several prominent citizens and business concerns were approached. Without exception they all thought it a lunatic venture but, for one reason or another, guardedly went along with it. There was one proviso. The railroad company had to agree to co-operate. If there was to be any profit in it, there had to be thousands of people there to watch. To get them there the Great Western Railway had to lay on special excursion trains.

The company sent three of their senior men, Messrs Vibbard, Gray and Collamer, to meet Blondin, Colcord and several important local people to see what was in it for the railway.

They met on the suspension bridge which spanned the gorge about a mile below the Falls. It had been opened four years before and the GWR had hopes of the vast traffic it would generate. They advertised it as 'The Only Route via Niagara Falls'. It was possible to see the Falls, but nowhere near as clearly as the posters made out. It had an upper deck for the trains and a lower deck for pedestrians and horsedrawn vehicles.

The railroad company men were not enthusiastic about Blondin's plan. They clearly doubted the possibility of the feat being accomplished and foresaw the probability of the company being put to a lot of expense only to have the whole thing called off at the last moment. Harry Colcord worked very hard trying to convince them. He listed his client's many achievements on both sides of the Atlantic. He had to agree that none of them really compared to what was now proposed.

The party was already edging its way towards the end of the bridge. Blondin decided to give them a demonstration. Dressed in his ordinary clothes, he calmly climbed over the bridge railing and lowered himself down one of the supports to the lower deck. He moved along to the point where one of the longest of the steel cable guys stretched down to the river bank far below. Easing himself on to the cable, then releasing his hold on the bridge girders, he began to walk down the steeply angled guy, balancing himself with his arms. On reaching the rock anchorage, he turned, climbed back up again and joined them on the upper deck without saying a word.

One of the prominent citizens, Mr Hamblin, gave the 1,300 dollars for the rope.

General Porter, the owner of Goat Island, was not prepared to allow any part of his land to be used for Blondin's enterprise. It was his father who had allowed Sam Patch to build his tower there but the General said he had no wish 'to be a party to anyone else's drowning'. No amount of persuasion, even from some of the prominent citizens, who were now behind the project, would change his mind.

This was a major setback; the embargo effectively ruled out a crossing of either the Horseshoe or the American Falls.

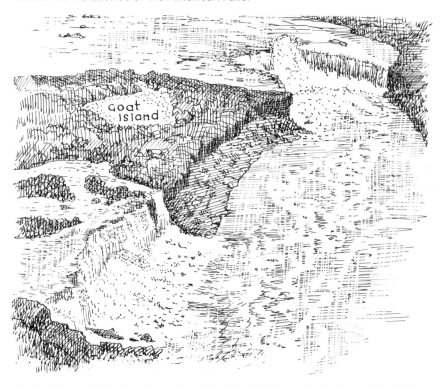

Blondin was bitterly disappointed. In his mind's eye he had seen his bridge only in one position – from Terrapin Point to Table Rock. A fall there would mean certain death and Blondin was sufficient of a showman to know that this was the factor which would draw the crowds.

Offering the maximum hazards, the site was the most challenging to his skill. A crossing anywhere else would be comparatively straightforward to a man of his capabilities. He had shown the equivalent by walking up and down the bridge guy and for that he hadn't bothered to change his clothes. The temptation to abandon the event was very great but by then too much was at stake and too many people were involved. If he withdrew at this stage, who would believe that it wasn't fear that had made him do so?

There was no alternative. He would find another site and go through with the idea as best he could.

An offer was made by Mr White, who owned pleasure gardens about half-way between the suspension bridge and the American Falls. He would allow the rope to be fixed on his land, enclose an area of the gardens, charge 25 cents admission and share the proceeds with Blondin on a 50/50 basis. The owners of the land on the Canadian side opposite were agreeable to the rope being fixed but made no demand to share the proceeds.

Blondin had several objections to White's proposition. The site was over a mile from the Horseshoe Falls and by the time the river reached there it had lost most of its turbulence. As the rope would be close enough to the bridge, this would be the best viewing point, and not the gardens.

For Blondin the whole thing had gone terribly wrong.

And, nothing could be done about it, the bandwaggon was rolling; newspapers, posters, railway hoardings and handbills all proclaimed 'Blondin will cross Niagara Falls on a tightrope'. Railway and coach ticket offices were already taking bookings even though a date had still to be fixed.

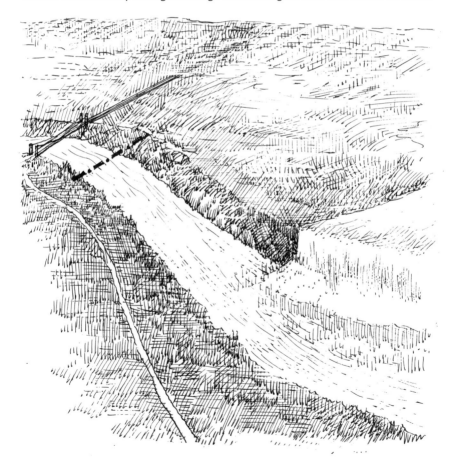

Although it was June it snowed at Niagara Falls in that month in 1859; great flakes fell as though it was winter.

It was an unwelcome sight down at the *Maid of the Mist* landing opposite the American Falls. The boat had only commenced operation for the new season the week before. The river often remained frozen over until the end of May, which made it a very short tourist season during which to carry passengers right to the foot of the Horseshoe Falls.

The company was still in financial difficulties from the disaster which occurred during a similar unexpected snowstorm eight years before. The first little steamer to bear the name was moored at the landing and became so top heavy with snow that she overturned and sank. Because of the risks undertaken in the normal way of her trade, no insurance company would consider any form of cover. The replacement was a much larger and costlier vessel and was still far from being paid for.

Before the suspension bridge was built, the only way across the river was by the ferry which had been started by Forsyth over thirty years before. Originally the ferry boats were rowed across. In 1846 the first steamer was launched. As the tourist trade built up, the owner found it more profitable running passenger trips close to the Falls. The bridge completely ruined the ferry business. The season was short and the overheads very high. Anything which would boost business was good news down at the landing.

Reading of Blondin's proposal did much to cheer Captain Joel E. Robinson, his crew and every member of the company.

Maid of the Mist comes from Indian legend. The Neutrals believed that the thunder god, Hinum, lived with his two sons in a cave behind the Horseshoe Falls. Each year a canoe filled with fruit and game was sent over the Falls as an appeasement sacrifice. At one period, many of the tribe were dying from an unknown cause; their graves were desecrated and the bodies devoured. It was felt that the gods were dissatisfied with the gifts and it was decided to sacrifice their most beautiful maiden.

One year it was the Chief's daughter who was the most beautiful. Her father watched the preparations, without sign of emotion, but when the canoe was sent on its way he set out after her in his own canoe. Both passed over the brink never to be seen again.

In the next two weeks the topic created controversy and argument.

'BLONDIN IS A FOOL WHO OUGHT TO BE ARRESTED'
New York Times

'HE WILL DO IT WITH AS LITTLE DIFFICULTY AS HE WOULD WALK A QUARTER OF A MILE ON A RACE TRACK'
New York Tribune

'THERE IS NO DOUBT THE FEAT WILL BE ACCOMPLISHED', said *St Catherine's Journal*, but warned . . .

'Every arrangement has been made by the people around the Falls to fleece all who attend of their dimes.
   Whiskey, confectionery, candy and other kinds of shops are going up in great numbers . . . Hoteliers, carriage proprietors and similar are getting their hair, whiskers, tongues and persons in a state to enable them to personate gentlemen'

   The *Niagara Mail*, a rival of the *Daily Gazette*, was slow in getting the news, only announcing it some three weeks after their competitor. They chose to be sarcastic . . .

'BARON MÜNCHAUSEN HAS EVIDENTLY COME TO LIFE AGAIN AND TAKEN UP HIS ABODE AT THE FALLS'
(The baron was a Russian cavalry officer, notorious for telling tall stories).

The editor treated the event trivially . . .

'Doubtless from the same manufactory is a story circulated through the press of a man having walked across the rapids on stilts' (there had been a well documented report of some Indians doing that) and he summed the whole thing up as 'circulated in the hope of drawing a crowd of simpletons for the benefit of the tribe of land sharks and imposters who live by tricks on travellers at Niagara Falls.'

The *Gazette*'s leader offered . . .

'to lend him (the editor of the *Niagara Mail*) a gun, and station sharpshooters to guard him from the land sharks, etcetera . . . What a fellow!'

The *Journal and Courier* said it would . . .
'send a reporter to write Blondin's obituary.'

The Clifton Hotel, at the head of the Ferry Road on the Canadian side of the river, offered a grandstand view of the crossing. Those guests with a balcony would pay a premium price. As a general principle the management usually disapproved of events of this kind. The Clifton was a high class establishment and the type of patrons who stayed there tended to regard this kind of thing as devaluing the town's chief asset, its natural beauty. However, with 150 bedrooms with full width balconies it was too good an opportunity for the hotel proprietor to miss.

All hotels and houses which had rooms overlooking the place suddenly found they were in great demand.

Thousands of people had no need to pay anything at all for a good view. The whole Front was wide open and free.

After several delays the rope was finally delivered by rail on 22 June. The two bundles were off-loaded at the American end of the suspension bridge and loaded on to a cart. Someone stuck a flag on top. It was not reported what kind of flag; the important thing was to have a flag. There was also an impromptu parade through the town to White's gardens and a sailor, who happened to be visiting, was given the job of splicing the two lengths of rope together.

At the point on the American bank where the rope was to be suspended, it was 160 feet (48.4m) above water and on the Canadian side, 170 feet (51.5m). The distance between the fixings was just over 1,100 feet (333.3m) in a direct line, but the weight would cause the rope to sag. Blondin had estimated it at 50 feet (15.2m), but it was in fact 60 feet (18.2m) with a gradient of 1 in 10, and consequently a fairly steep slope.

The first stage in the fixing was to get a light line across the river. Several attempts to do this in the next few days all failed as the lines broke. It required one nearly an inch thick to be strong enough to take the strain. Two men in a rowing boat began the crossing half a mile upstream because of the fast flowing current. It was a heavy task with the rope dragging in the water. Once across, it was passed through a pulley and on to a windlass ready to haul the main 3¼ inch rope.

They began hauling. It was necessary to keep the main rope reasonably taut to avoid it drooping into the river and to minimise the weight to be borne by the lighter rope. The possibility of its breaking caused anxiety as more and more of the heavy rope was paid out. When the looped end was within almost 300 feet (90.9m) of the Canadian bank, Blondin thought that unless something was done, failure was certain. Tying the end of another rope round his waist, he gave instructions for two men to pay out the line as he crawled out on to the winch line, drawing himself along with his hands and feet. The unstayed rope swung alarmingly and his weight caused it to sag, until his body was at an angle over the sheer drop. Had the line parted, he would have swung back against the rock face, without hope of survival. It took a long time to reach the main rope, but he eventually reached the loop, secured the additional line and edged his way back to the shore. The crowd of spectators applauded this unrehearsed exhibition of his skill. With the double support, the hauling was soon completed.

The final stage was the guying of the rope to give it stability. Blondin insisted on doing this personally. It meant going across on a small box attached to the main rope. It had grooved wheels, but would not run by itself. He had to crawl along the rope for about 20 feet (6.0m) and fix a pulley through which a rope passed back to the box. An assistant hauled the box to a position close to Blondin and he climbed down to fix the guy. Then the whole operation had to be repeated until all the twenty nine guys on the Canadian side, and twenty five on the American were in position. This left a length of about 40 feet (12.0m) between the middle two. After that, the whole system was tensioned and the guys secured. Everything was now ready and a date was fixed for 30 June.

Crowds, variously estimated at 10,000–25,000 people, went to Niagara Falls that day. Mayor Cornwall and the Corporation of Clifton, on the Canadian side, were concerned that, in the crush on the river bank, persons would be pushing each other over the edge and hurriedly arranged for a strong barred fence to be put up. A man had fallen over the previous day.

The Great Western, New York Central, Erie and the Ontario & Lewiston Railway Companies all laid on extra trains.

The Arrow steamer carried 500 passengers from Buffalo, across Lake Erie to the Canadian shore. From there they travelled by road and rail down through Chippawa to the Falls.

The steamship *Zimmerman,* named after the founder of Clifton, sailed from Toronto, across Lake Ontario to Niagara on the Lake, from where the passengers travelled past the great whirlpool, to the suspension bridge. Blondin had appeared at the Toronto Lyceum the previous year and had a lot of admirers in that city.

Almost overnight a large number of stands for spectators appeared along the Front, most of them built by private individuals with 'an eye for the fast buck'. Many were rickety and unsafe.

The weather was sunny and without a breeze. Ideal from Blondin's point of view, but many spectators crowded together found it too hot.

Niagara Falls took on a carnival aspect, but the reporters said 'the crowd was well behaved' and regarded it as being 'a sign of the times that hardly a single person was seen to be under the influence of liquor'. Perhaps they couldn't afford the recent rapidly inflated prices.

An open barouche arrived at the entrance to the enclosure in White's gardens. It was festooned with the flags of France, America, Canada and Britain. Placards on the sides announced that this was 'The Great Blondin', and he stood up to acknowledge the applause. Over his fleshings he wore a purple velvet vest, white Turkish pantaloons and on his head a brightly coloured cap attached to a curly wig. Pointed oriental sandals protected his buckskin slippers, to protect them until he was ready to step on to the rope.

A number of 'blacklegs' were among the crowd, pickpockets, card-sharps, and 'con-men' of various kinds. The Clifton Police had many reports of wallets, purses, cash and valuables changing hands that day in 'one sided bargains', with little or no prospect of recovery.

Some of the would-be spectators spent the time in saloons, bars or upstairs rooms in and around the area, never seeing the event they had come to Niagara Falls especially to view.

At three o'clock, a cannon was fired in White's Pleasure Gardens to announce that proceedings were about to commence. Those who had been tempted away to see the Falls or some of the other attractions began to converge. Observers noted that there were twice as many people on the Canadian side, where viewing was free. Only about 4,000 paid the 25 cents to go inside White's enclosure, inspite of the announcement that Blondin would perform a few feats on a tightrope set up within the gardens.

Not to be outdone, a cannon had been brought out on the Canadian shore; it was called Old Lundy and had been captured at the battle. When the time came, it was loaded with a blank charge and a match put to the touch hole. Nothing happened. Three attempts were made to fire it. All failed. It was trundled back to the museum to the jeers of the crowd.

Shortly after five o'clock, Blondin appeared at the end of the rope and for the first time came into view of the main body of spectators.

Although Blondin was of medium height, the thin heel-less slippers made him appear shorter than his 5 feet 8 inches (1.7m). At 142 pounds (64.5 kgs), his build was stocky and the close-fitting fleshings emphasised the broad chest and muscular arms. Around his waist was a short brightly coloured skirt, with a decorated border, held by a studded belt. A wide loose collar draped round his shoulders and down on to his chest. Though not the blonde colour that had earned his father's nickname, Blondin's hair was fair and swept over the ears to the nape of his neck. A full and droopy moustache wrapped round a short pointed beard, as favoured by Napoleon III and named Imperial.

The *Tribune*'s reporter described him as having 'light gray eyes, very keen and piercing, and the manner of a man perfectly self-possessed, and with the most complete confidence in himself'.

There is no doubt about this. In many ways he regarded the feat he was about to perform as being almost contemptibly easy. To him, a rope over three inches (75mm) thick was like a race track. He was used to a thinner rope.

As he looked upstream to the Horseshoe Falls, the perfectionist in him resented the absence of challenge in the present location. As he looked at the water below, he compared it to the white broiling foam at the foot of the Falls and the disappointment bit into him again. He was an artist and knew that what he was about to do was a mere extension of what he had done before.

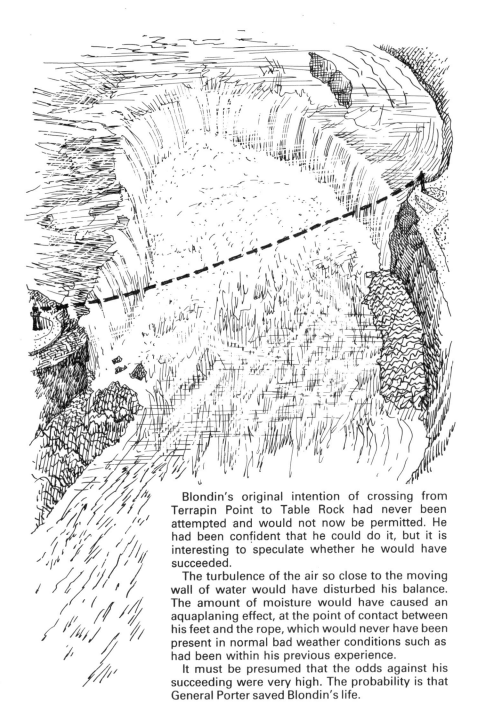

Blondin's original intention of crossing from Terrapin Point to Table Rock had never been attempted and would not now be permitted. He had been confident that he could do it, but it is interesting to speculate whether he would have succeeded.

The turbulence of the air so close to the moving wall of water would have disturbed his balance. The amount of moisture would have caused an aquaplaning effect, at the point of contact between his feet and the rope, which would never have been present in normal bad weather conditions such as had been within his previous experience.

It must be presumed that the odds against his succeeding were very high. The probability is that General Porter saved Blondin's life.

At five fifteen precisely on the 30 June 1859 Blondin became the first to attempt a crossing of the Niagara gorge on a tightrope. He carried a balancing pole, about 30 feet (9.0m) long and weighted with lead to about 40 pounds. Before he set off, he looked round the crowd and announced, in the broken French accent he never lost, that he was about 'to make the ascension'. Then he made an offer: 'Gentlemen, any one what please to across, I carry him on my back'. No one seemed disposed to accept. One shouted 'Goodbye!'. Another 'Leave us a lock of your hair to remember you by!'. The reporter of the *Lockport Journal & Courier* pressed forward to say he had come to write Blondin's obituary and was there anything to add. He was thanked politely for coming but informed there was no intention of providing him with any such item.

With a final enquiry 'No one?' and a shrug of his shoulders, Blondin stepped out. Within a few paces, the bank fell away and he was 150 feet (45.4m) above the river.

Mr Corning, of the railroad company, had not been slow to realise that the change of venue made the suspension bridge a ready-made grandstand. An excursion train of precisely the right length, which happened to stop on the bridge at the right moment, suddenly had the potential for very special excursion rates and opportunities for 'V.I.P.' treatment for the selected few. The lower pedestrian deck provided space for an enormous number of paying customers.

The *Maid of the Mist* was packed with passengers, and very low in the water, as she left her mooring. It would be some years before Samuel Plimsoll's line appeared on the sides of vessels to prevent overloading. Captain Robinson was happy at the sight of so many passengers wishing to pay special rates to be out on the river under Blondin's rope. He'd had the idea that a bottle of wine should be carried on board, and when Blondin reached the halfway point he would lower a light line and haul up the bottle for a drink. Blondin agreed, providing it was a non-alcoholic beverage in keeping with his lifelong teetotal principles. At five o'clock on the day, the paddle steamer was in position, head into the current. All eyes on board turned upwards as the tiny figure appeared against the sky 150 feet (45.4m) above them.

The *Lockport Daily Advertiser & Democrat* reporter remained sufficiently detached to watch crowd reaction rather than the performance itself:

'A noticeable circumstance was the silence that pervaded the host of spectators. It was like the hushed stillness of the forest during a lull of the winds. Not a voice was heard not even a word of encouragement: people were holding their breath, absorbed in the result. So intently engaged was the mind, that we have our doubts whether there was even one who heard the roar of the cataract which was thundering on the ear ... A similar emotion prevails among large masses while contemplating the peril of a fellow being on a rock in the rapids, on witnessing a shipwreck, or while waiting the result of a battle and the pending victory.'

A similar detachment was displayed by the pickpockets, who also gave their attention to the crowd and not the performance. Among the losses reported was one of a gold watch, a wallet containing 300 dollars and a pocket book with 80 dollars. One lady lost a portmannie, which she was carrying at the time, and the 35 dollars inside. A particularly cautious man placed a knife in the same pocket as his purse; he later found blood on the knife blade, but the purse was gone.

Not one single arrest was made.

An old lady from the country said: 'How much faith Blondin must have in ...', pointing her parasol meaningfully to the sky. Then, filled with guilt, she confessed to all around her 'I haven't got a bit'.

White had seen to it that a band was on the American shore to play Blondin on his way, and as he set out along the rope they struck up with *On the Other Side of Jordan* — nobody had found time to compose a tune called '*On the Other Side of Niagara*'. The bandmaster thought the reference to a river of some sort was adequate. Very few people were listening, the band was only there to add to the carnival; an addition to the flags, bunting, lanterns and streamers.

On the other shore a similar band was waiting. Their music cards were *Home Sweet Home*. Their bandmaster thought that would be an appropriate tune to welcome him ashore. Just in case, they also had cards for *Get Out of the Wilderness*.

Blondin took his time to get used to the incline and feel of the rope and it took him three minutes to walk the first 100 feet (30.3m). There he stopped. The crowd wondered if something had gone wrong. The band lost its rhythm, then ceased playing altogether. All eyes were on the stationary figure out there beyond any form of assistance. Then, with the ease of reclining on a bed, he slowly lay down with his back on the rope, crossed his legs and stretched out.

Having rested for a little while he stood up and moved forward for another 100 feet (30.3m), stopped again and stood on one leg. A gasp went up from the crowd. Vaguely imagining themselves in the same position, they had assumed that once on the rope it would be a rush to the other side to get off it again as quickly as possible. This kind of leisurely progress was totally unexpected. There were some rowing boats in the river below him; Blondin seemed to find these interesting and sat down to view them with obvious enjoyment.

Arriving above the *Maid of the Mist*, he sat down again, laid the pole across the rope and placed one knee over it to preserve his balance and prevent it falling into the river. From around his waist he uncoiled a length of light string and lowered it to the deck of the steamer. Captain Robinson was torn between his duty to command the vessel and his desire to be the one who participated in an historic event, but decided the overloaded vessel had first call on his services. A member of the crew was given the job of tying the bottle to the string and giving the signal on which Blondin hoisted it, took a refreshing drink and lowered it back to the waiting crewman below. This took another seven minutes, after which he proceeded safely to the Canadian shore.

The band had sufficiently recovered its discipline to play *Auld Lang Syne* as the drink was taken at the centre point. The Canadian band got its cards mixed up and instead of playing *Home Sweet Home* greeted him with *Get Out of the Wilderness*.

It had taken seventeen and a-half minutes to complete the whole crossing.

On both banks, crowds cheered and bands played. White's cannon boomed out its congratulations as fast as it could be reloaded. Old Lundy's failure to fire was a bitterly resented let-down to Canadian prestige.

Many more wallets, purses and valuables changed hands in the excitement of the moment.

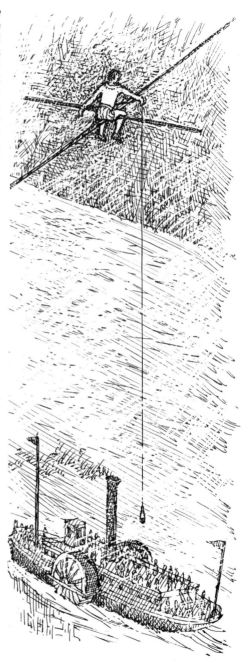

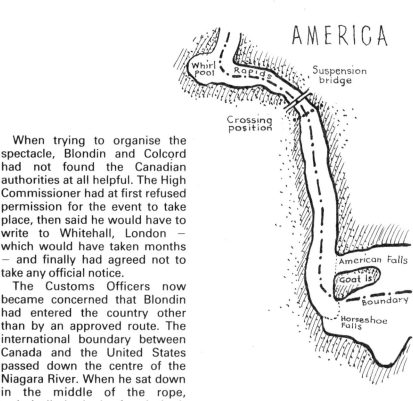

AMERICA

Whirl pool

Rapids

Suspension bridge

Crossing position

American Falls

Goat Is

Boundary

Horseshoe Falls

CANADA

When trying to organise the spectacle, Blondin and Colcord had not found the Canadian authorities at all helpful. The High Commissioner had at first refused permission for the event to take place, then said he would have to write to Whitehall, London — which would have taken months — and finally had agreed not to take any official notice.

The Customs Officers now became concerned that Blondin had entered the country other than by an approved route. The international boundary between Canada and the United States passed down the centre of the Niagara River. When he sat down in the middle of the rope, technically he had a foot in both countries and had entered Canada without completing the necessary formalities. It was not a matter to be treated lightly. A precedent had been set which others might follow.

Harry Colcord was on the Canadian side to welcome him. In his excitement he went out on to the rope a few feet, hurriedly returning when he realised where he was.

A group calling themselves 'The Friends of Blondin' made a collection round the hotels, which realised 300 dollars. The 'Sons of Malta' put a purse together for him, it being rumoured he was a member. Blondin received these two contributions, but many other hats and collecting boxes went among the crowd, into which dollars and cents were tossed, which were not passed to him.

Everybody was amazed when, after a short rest, Blondin announced he was returning to the American side on the rope.

Captain Robinson was furious when he looked up from the landing and saw what was happening. He had returned, triumphantly waving the wine bottle, happy that he had been present on a historic one-off occasion. Had he known, he would have been out there with a fresh load of fee-paying passengers.

The American band had put down their instruments, once Blondin was on his way, and become spectators. The Canadian band had begun to pack up, when they hurriedly had to unpack and get into some sort of order to play him away again with *Yankee Doodle Dandy*.

By comparison with the outward journey, the return was almost too straightforward. It was all over in seven minutes. He stopped only once to sit down and wave.

Mr Kavanagh of the Great Western Hotel had laid on champagne, not knowing that Blondin was teetotal, but there were plenty of people who were not. Cigars were handed round by others, who didn't know that Blondin was a non-smoker, but plenty of others smoked.

Shoulder high, Blondin was carried back to the flag-draped barouche and paraded through the streets back to the Old Falls Hotel.

Newspaper presses all over the country were printing the name that soon would be known to millions. Cables carried the news to Europe.

The reports were followed quickly by a confusing array of contradictions. One cable contained a positive denial that any such person as Blondin existed and denounced the whole thing as a publicity stunt by the hoteliers of Niagara Falls. It subsequently turned out to have been sent by the hoteliers of Newport, in an attempt to safeguard their own business.

Madame Blondin had stayed in Cincinnati to await the arrival of their child and was not present to see his triumph.

The proceeds were counted next day. Those finding their way into Blondin's own pocket were disappointingly low. Only about 1,000 people out of the 4,000 watching went into White's Pleasure Gardens and paid the 25 cents admission, so his share amounted to 250 dollars. With the 300 dollars collected by the Friends and purse from the Sons of Malta, together with other small takings, the total sum received by Blondin amounted to 600 dollars. This may have seemed a good day's pay, but it had represented a full month's work.

There were hotel bills to pay. Harry Colcord was entitled to his ten percent. Costumes had been bought, carriages hired and there were boat charges and oarsmen. Even though Mr Hamblin paid for the rope, four men over four days were paid for fixing it into position. As a financial venture it could not be regarded as a great success. If there was to be any profit, the performance would have to be repeated again and again.

The next performance was fixed for 4 July. On the American side this would be Independence Day, which would increase the holiday crowds. A 'new angle' suggested by Blondin made the other two shudder at the thought; he would go across tied in a sack. To the layman, this obliteration of the senses of sight and sound appeared suicidal, but Blondin knew the only sense that he relied on was touch; his sensitive feet would still be able to feel the rope. He explained all this to them but they remained sceptical. To Blondin the perfectionist, this was a new 'handicap' to challenge his ability, and he remained adamant. The other two had to agree it was certainly a spectacular new development.

To cater for 'the carriage trade' it was decided to build seating in the enclosure, for which an additional 25 cents would be charged. It was hoped that this touch of luxury and comfort would attract a wealthier type of customer.

42

Word had got around that there were rich pickings to be had and the opportunists were out in force on the 4th July ...

In Niagara Falls, on both sides, the liquor purveyors knew that people would get hot and require liquid refreshment. A large number of ladies would be there and lemonade would be in big demand, with escorts not wishing to query the price. The drink was made with water and the tiniest quantity of tartaric acid. At a dollar a glass it valued tartaric acid at 500 dollars a pound, some 2,000% up on its real price. Buckshot Whiskey was also popular and similarly expensive.

More and more spectator stands were built, and this time they were situated in a position where they blocked the view from areas which had been free vantage points for the previous performance.

On every available site, booths sprang up offering all manner of souvenirs, gimmicks, viewing aids and mementoes. Had all the locks of hair come from Blondin's head, he would have been completely bald. Pieces of the 'actual rope' were on sale, despite the actual rope being there for all to see. A number of the visual aids were found to impede vision, rather than assist, due to the lenses being ordinary bottle glass.

In spite of all expectations, the crowds on the 4 July were not noticeably greater than on the 30 June.

A major criticism to be heard all round was the lack of lavatory accommodation, especially for the ladies. White had attempted to alleviate the problem for his 'carriage trade' customers, but the arrangements were far from adequate.

A few minutes before five o'clock Blondin appeared at the end of the main rope. He started out by walking backwards, and went out for about 75 feet (22.7m). He then returned because the tension had slackened and was not to his liking. Adjustments were made to the guys and he set off again. At about 150 feet (45.4m) he repeated his one legged stance. Moving forward about the same distance again he lay down to 'have a snooze'. Proceeding towards the centre the pole became entangled with one of the guys and it seemed that he would lose his balance. There was a gasp of anticipation from the crowd but he succeeded in extricating the pole and continued to the Canadian shore, stopping for another 'siesta' at the three-quarter position. The time taken for the whole crossing was eight and a half minutes.

44

Yielding to pressure from Colcord, White and many wellwishers, Blondin agreed not to use an ordinary sack for his crossing but improvised one from a large Indian blanket. This allowed his feet to be free and in close contact with the rope. His arms were also on the outside to give a better grip on the balancing pole. In spite of these modifications, there were protests from the American side that the 'sack' made it too dangerous. Fearing that the authorities might take steps to forbid the performance, the blanket was taken over to the Canadian bank.

After resting for an hour or so on the Canadian side, Blondin commenced his return journey in the 'sack'. He may have experienced some difficulty at the start because a reporter on the bank said he proceeded with much more caution and his legs appeared to be trembling. Soon he was stepping out with confidence and the American shore was reached in ten minutes. His arrival was greeted with such a clamour of cheering, train whistles, bands and cannon fire that it was impossible for people to hear themselves speak. Again he was carried shoulder high to his carriage and paraded through the streets to his hotel.

Financial results were not as high as had been hoped and expected. Celebrations at Lockport, Buffalo and elsewhere were partly to blame. Blondin, Colcord and White did as well, or as badly, as they had the first time, but were well aware they were receiving only a fraction of the wealth they were creating.

The next performance, the third, was fixed for 14 July. France's National Day.

45

Captain Robinson of the *Maid of the Mist* introduced Captain Travis from Louisville, who had a considerable reputation as a pistol shot. He was easily persuaded to take part in a scheme that would do them both a bit of good. They had more difficulty in persuading Blondin to agree and Harry Colcord was totally against the idea. Finally, they accepted the proposition. Again it was to be at the time of Blondin's arrival at the centre.

The *Maid of the Mist,* in position below, had Captain Travis on deck with a loaded revolver. At a given signal he would shoot a hole through a hat held by Blondin. This was mutually agreed to be too dangerous and the trick was modified to the hat being lowered on a short line. The two captains were delighted to have their scheme approved. They might well be as both had everything to gain and nothing to lose.

On the other hand Blondin had everything to lose. At worst it could have been his life. At best he was handing over a substantially profitable participation in his act at no cost to the captains whatsoever. Harry should have known better but, in fairness to him, this kind of activity was outside his experience. He was also feeling aggrieved. Things had moved so quickly and his client often did things without consulting him. Having secured a contract for Blondin to resume his former career by joining Franconi's Circus at a high fee, he wanted this crossing to be the last, but he was overruled.

Captain Robinson came up with the next 'new angle'. He had been disappointed at not being included in the second crossing. He had seen to it that the *Maid of the Mist* was loaded to capacity and made two trips to profit from both the outward and return journeys but he missed the added prestige of taking part, as he had with the wine drinking act, and was determined to get back into the proceedings.

In view of the shooting proposal a number of extra guys were added to give greater stability and a steadier target for Captain Travis.

The preliminaries followed the same pattern as on the previous two occasions. A quarter of the way across Blondin sat down to have a rest, then went on to the centre where he sat down again. A hat was lowered on a string to hang about twenty feet (6m) below him and slightly to one side.

46

The *Maid of the Mist,* crowded again, was cruising in the vicinity and now Robinson brought her into position as directed by Travis with the full dramatic intensity the occasion demanded. Finally he called 'Hold her steady!' With all the flair and showmanship that had established his reputation, he drew the revolver, took careful aim and fired. Then he blew into the barrel in the manner of the crackshot, replaced the gun in its holster and signalled Blondin to lower the hat to the deck.

There was a hole through the centre of the crown. The applause on deck was spontaneous and admiring.

There appeared to be no doubt in anybody's mind that the hole in the hat was made by the bullet from Captain Travis's gun.

His reputation was as a pistol shot. With only one exception, and that from a newspaper which said it was relying on a report received, all stated categorically that it was a revolver that was used. To minimise the risk to Blondin, the shot was not fired from a position directly underneath him, which would have been the shortest distance, but from a point where the line of fire would have passed underneath the rope. That distance was variously quoted as between 250–300 feet (75.7–90.0m). The pistol is essentially a short range weapon, the lead ball is not designed to give accurate flight over long distances. Most crackshot demonstrations take place at a range of about 90 feet (27.3m).

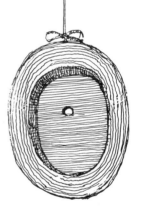

On the strength of the publicity he received for this display, Travis opened a shooting gallery in Lockport which was reported to be 'daily thronged' with men anxious to learn from him how to shoot the pistol.

No prior examination of the hat seems to have taken place. Perhaps if it had . . .

Blondin reached the Canadian shore some seventeen minutes after setting out. He had rested again some hundred feet out from the bank but seemed to be exhausted on arrival. Perspiration covered his body with moisture but he was in good spirits, and shook hands with all around him before being escorted to a carriage and taken to the Clifton Hotel, to refesh himself for the return trip.

At five thirty five p.m., a closed carriage drew up close by the rope on the Canadian side. The crowd anticipated Blondin's return from the Clifton Hotel and gathered round. To their amazement 'a fair representation of an immense baboon' stepped out of the carriage. A man standing by described it later to the *Toronto Spectator* reporter as 'a hideous looking object, impossible to conceive anything more hideous. Looks like the Devil!'. The reporter added that 'never having seen that personage, I am unable to say whether there is a family resemblance or not'. It did not take the crowd long to realise it was another of Blondin's tricks. Having crossed in a sack, he was now going to do so dressed as an ape.

The 'ape' reached back inside the carriage and took out a wheelbarrow. It was purpose-made from whitewood with a broad grooved wheel, to fit on the rope. It weighed between 20 and 30 pounds (9.0 and 13.6kg) and was brightly and decoratively painted. Thomas Duncan, the stage carpenter at the Buffalo Theatre, had made it to Blondin's requirements.

The barrow was trundled to the rope and the grooved wheel placed on to it. Blondin fitted the handles into loops at the waist of his costume. With a wave he set off, pushing the barrow in front of him with his body and carrying the balancing pole in his hands. This time he could not rest; the heavy costume hindered his progress and it was insufferably hot. The return to the American shore was completed in eleven minutes.

At the end of the third performance, the crowds quickly dispersed and there were fewer transport delays. A better organised collection realised over 1,000 dollars and covered all expenses with a profit of 518 dollars.

Just before it got dark an Englishman, who was a gardener in the employ of Mr Barnett, the proprietor of the Niagara Falls museum, went down the old wooden steps that had formerly led to the ferry landing. He walked along the river bank until he arrived under Blondin's rope. No one else was close by him but many people were still on both banks, wondering why he was there. Taking off his jacket and shoes the man entered the water and began to swim across. The water surface, though quick flowing, appeared relatively calm and for a time progress was steady. Underneath, there are powerful currents which rotate, from the action of the American Falls, and it is about 200 feet deep at that position. The swimmer suddenly disappeared. His body was never found. What he was trying to prove remained a mystery.

The success of Blondin's latest exhibition, and the size of the crowd, made the Americans even more determined to get him to the Upper Falls of the Genessee. He was told that there would be no hindrances at Rochester; there would be a pre-arranged fee and a cut of all the profits.

A young Rochester man, Henry L. Young, aged twenty four, offered to be a passenger in Blondin's barrow or on his back.

The offers were tempting, but Blondin had other things on his mind. He left Niagara next morning and travelled to Cincinnati. Charlotte had given birth to their second daughter on 10 July.

They called their new daughter Iris and decided to move to Niagara Falls. A house was rented on Third Street; not far from White's Pleasure Gardens.

Things could not have gone better for the *Daily Gazette* in the first month of publication. They had given their editorial backing to Blondin, even though it had been a safe thing to do, as they had 'hedged the bet' so that they could have said 'told you so' whether he succeeded or failed.

The *Niagara City Herald* had chosen to ignore the whole matter from the beginning. When it repeatedly became fact, the *Herald* was the only paper with no report on a topic that was on everybody's lips. On the last day of July, the editor decided that the best way of defence was attack. He sought to justify the neglect by saying there was nothing at all unusual in the feat and that a number of people were quite prepared to do the same.

Delighted, the *Gazette* gave the first day of August leader column the headline 'RIP VAN WINKLE AWAKES!'. The first line began 'The *Niagara City Herald* has just learned that there is such a man as Blondin; that he performs on a tightrope, indeed, that he has actually crossed the Niagara five or six times on a rope! Its readers will no doubt be astonished at the news and thank the enterprising editor for this exhibition of his desire to keep them posted on passing local events'. The *Gazette* piled sarcasm on sarcasm. 'This isn't all! The enterprising editor has been round taking notes, and declares that the press, and especially *THE GAZETTE* ... (the name was in large type and heavily underlined) ... has a good deal to say about BLONDIN ...' (again the name was set in heavy type and underlined). 'Singular that the papers should say anything about such a common occurrence as walking over the Niagara on a rope, when the *Herald* says nary a word!'.

The *Herald* had said: 'If it was known, there are several Italian and French rope walkers who could perform the same thing'. The *Gazette* retorted: 'What a pity it isn't known!'

After defending their original support for Blondin, the *Gazette* denied the paper was 'an organ for him or anybody else'. The attack was 'Uncalled for and unjust!. It is proper for the public to understand the animus of the writer.'

The Times (London) made no comment on the crossings until after the third one had been successfully completed. A cable was despatched on 30 June, as soon as Blondin reached the Canadian side for the first time. By the time any mention was made at all, he had made the double crossing twice more. It was given the barest coverage of not more than fifty words.

On 18 July, *The Times* commented on the subject: 'Extraordinary feat. One that fits the performer for the highest place in the lunatic asylum.'

Other papers were calling it an achievement. *The Times* would have none of this. 'When you reflect that the distance is so great that, with all care, the slack of the rope made a descent of 60 feet (16.3m) at the centre, and that a single false step must have plunged him to certain death in the current that runs with a rapidity which defies the sounding lead, you can have some idea of the difficulties and dangers and can appreciate the foolhardiness of the man who did such a feat.'

Neither Blondin nor White was satisfied with the present 50/50 arrangement. Both wanted more. The performer because he considered he was the attraction and had the skill. The impresario because he had paid out money and thought the return too little.

It did not seem that an agreement was going to be possible and Blondin began to take down his rope. After a few guys had been removed, they decided to have one more try, as everything was in place. A 'Final Performance' was announced for 3 August.

The largest crowd yet, estimated at 5,000 more than any previous appearance, turned out to see this event. It was decided that this would be a race against a boat. Blondin on his rope, a rowing boat across the old ferry route. At the signal, he set off at a trot and the boat left the landing on the American side. The crowd was cheering for Blondin. He would probably have completed the journey in three and a half minutes, but several times the pole caught in the guys. As it was, he crossed in six minutes, well ahead of the boat.

After a short rest on the Canadian side, Blondin set out on the return journey. Moving to the centre, he tied his balancing pole on to the main rope and performed a number of tricks without it.

He hung from the rope with his hands; by his feet; one foot; one hand.

From a one hand hold he drew himself parallel to the rope and outwards at right angles to it. Finally he climbed back up, lay on his stomach and went through the motions of swimming.

The crowd loved it. When he reached the American side people rushed forward to congratulate him. Money was pressed into his hands. A speech was called for but he declined, pleading his poor command of English.

It had been a tremendous success. One thing was certain, this could not possibly be a 'Final Performance'. Something even more spectacular would have to be offered.

It was. Blondin announced that next time he would carry a man – unnamed – across on his back. The day would be in two weeks, on 17 August.

Harry Colcord applauded the showmanship of keeping the secret but did think that, as agent, he should have been taken into Blondin's confidence. It was gratifying to be assured that he would be the first to know. The pledge was kept, Harry was given the name on the day itself . . . 'Harry Colcord'! At first he laughed, thinking it was a joke. When he realised it wasn't he told Blondin he was mad. Finally he agreed to be carried.

In an interview towards the end of his life, Harry said he never knew to that day how he allowed himself to be persuaded. It is quite remarkable that a man who had never set foot on a tightrope — apart from the few unintentional steps in the excitement of the first crossing — would agree to such a proposal. Blondin was a professional; to him the present setting was only an extension of his previous experience, to an initiate the prospect must have been appalling.

If the gamblers had been uncertain on earlier crossings, they had no doubts about this one and the 'odds' were all against success. A great deal of money was placed; some bets were very substantial. On the Sunday before the event was due to take place, nine of the guy ropes were found to have been cut. Later, a fire was found burning under another. It looked as though somebody was trying to lengthen the odds.

Some newspapers, including the *Gazette,* were against Blondin's latest proposal. Some called for an official ban. As the opposition seemed to be on the American side, it was decided that Harry should be waiting on the Canadian bank.

There was a lighthearted report that the railway company were considering taking out an injunction preventing Blondin carrying a man across, on the grounds that the company was the only one licensed to transport passengers across the river.

The dust was suffocating and the only place said to be tolerable was at Table Rock where the spray cleared the atmosphere. 40,000 was the estimated number watching; the highest yet.

At a few minutes after four o'clock, Blondin set out from the American side. As the main attraction was to be the return walk, he didn't waste much time on the outward journey except to pretend he had forgotten something; he tied his pole to the rope and returned without it, then went back again to show he could manage perfectly well and did not really need the pole at all. After a few routine tricks he arrived at the Canadian shore.

Colcord was waiting, although there had been doubts that he would be. He was taller than Blondin and weighed three pounds more and so, with the pole, the load was 190 pounds (57.5kg). Blondin gave him instructions: he was to hold on only by his arms and keep his legs from becoming entangled with Blondin's. He was not to look down, or wriggle about. Another thing Harry had not been told was that they would need to rest. It was only when they were 100 feet (30.3m) out on the rope that he was told to climb down and actually stand on the rope himself, and hold on as best he could, in order to give Blondin time to recuperate. This had to be repeated five times during the crossing. Blondin had thought the dangerous moment would be as Harry climbed back again but this seemed to present no difficulty.

It took twenty two minutes to reach the half-way point. This was the easier downhill part of the journey yet they were both covered in perspiration and very tired.

After a short rest, they set off again but had not gone more than 10 feet (3.0m) when the rope suddenly jerked violently from side to side. Somebody was deliberately swinging on one of the outer guy ropes. For a moment it seemed inevitable that Blondin would lose his balance. He worked the balancing pole vigorously up and down and from side to side but it seemed certain they would fall. It was only by running forward that the situation was saved. They reached the first guy rope and stopped for Blondin to recover. He put his foot on to the guy but it snapped. They lurched forward and again it was only by running forward that balance was restored.

About 100 feet (30.3m) along the rope, Blondin called to Harry 'Descendez vous' and, after a few moments rest, he cheerfully said 'Allons!'. Harry climbed back up and they completed the crossing.

The crowd surged forward and they couldn't get off the rope. Beneath them the cliff fell away vertically for 100 feet (30.3m).

With great presence of mind, Blondin let his pole fall to his feet where it remained, lying across several of the guy ropes. He took hold of Harry's legs and charged into the crowd. The momentum carried them both to safety and a last minute disaster had been averted.

In the excitement of their arrival, one man picked up Harry as though he was a baby, held him aloft and shouted 'Thank God it's over!'. Harry no doubt shared the sentiment.

Many had turned away during the latter stages of the crossing, not daring to watch.

A few people had fainted.

The whole crossing had taken forty two minutes, more than three times as long as on any of the previous occasions.

This event gave Blondin his place in the history of human achievement.

He had carried a man, one and a half times his own weight, for a period of forty two minutes along 1,000 feet (302.0m) of narrow rope high above the water. The load was concentrated on a few muscles in his feet. His quick thinking in arduous conditions dealing with the totally unexpected crises distinguished him as a highly skilled athlete and unique performer. He had been the first to accomplish such a feat. Others who followed could only emulate the master.

Blondin made light of the rope-shaking incident and the guy breaking but Colcord, and many other people, remained convinced that it was a quite deliberate attempt by a gambler who had bet on failure. Many people testified to having seen a man holding one of the guy ropes down by the river's edge where it was secured, and to seeing him run away and hide among the dense undergrowth. On the second matter, a man was seen in the vicinity of the guy ropes with a knife in his hand. There could be a rational explanation for that, but the guy rope did appear to have been cut and had not broken. Both incidents were reported to the police, but there was little they could do.

The Paris newspapers got it all wrong and reported that Blondin had been killed trying to carry a man across Niagara Falls. In some detail they described his 'fall into the raging cataract' and stated that 'his body has not been discovered'.

This represented a common misconception. Blondin never crossed 'the raging cataract'. His crossings were more than half a mile from the Falls.

In retrospect, it would probably have been better if Blondin had made the crossing with Harry the finale, but three more events were organised.

On 24 August he went out as 'A Liberian Slave' with manacles on his hands and feet. Returning as a 'French Chef' he carried a cooking stove on his back, prepared some omelettes at the centre and lowered them to the passengers on the *Maid of the Mist.*

The 31 August was a night crossing; he had lamps on the ends of the pole, both of which went out leaving him to complete the crossing in total darkness.

On 8 September it was with a table and chair from which he ate cakes. The return was with his feet in baskets.

The appeal was diminishing. Only about 6,000 people turned out for the last performance, most of whom were non-payers.

The end of the 1859 season was celebrated with a series of receptions and parties at the Clifton House Hotel.

On 10 October, a group of about twenty of the prominent citizens who had backed him organised a party and asked Madame Blondin to take him there on the pretext of going out to dinner. After the meal a presentation was made. It was a gold medal, on one side of which was modelled a representation of Blondin on the tightrope; on the other was an engraved inscription reading:

'Presented to Mons. J.F. Blondin by the citizens of Niagara Falls N.Y. in appreciation of a feat never before attempted by man but by him successfully performed on 17 August 1859, that of carrying a man across the Falls of Niagara on a tightrope.'

Harry Colcord didn't receive a medal.

On 14 October, it was Charlotte's turn to have a surprise party. It was her birthday and Blondin made it appear that he had forgotten about it until the last moment when, instead of a meal at home she was taken by carriage to the Clifton for a large party.

Finally, the two of them held a reception which was very well attended. Blondin had a short length of tightrope put up in the ballroom on which he performed a number of comic tricks and as a finale carried his wife across on his back. She was described as being 'very graceful'.

Had he been a better businessman, Blondin would have held on to the money he had made. Other people were not prepared to risk their money and he should not have used his own. The following year, he decided to hire another site at his own expense. The only one he could find was on the other side of the suspension bridge. This was even further from the Falls but was directly above the rapids leading into the great whirlpool. A fall here was certain death but he did not consider that eventuality. The new location had all the problems of the previous one: the grandstand on the suspension bridge; the vast amount of space from which people could watch without paying; the absence of shade trees and the distance from the busy centre of the tourist trade – the Front.

A further example of his unbusinesslike approach was the outright purchase of 100,000 seats.

Putting up the rope was a great deal more costly in this position. It was impossible to row a boat across the rapids, the line had to be carried upstream to the bridge, across that and back down the opposite bank. Guying was much more difficult and the whole operation had to be paid for by Blondin. There was no Mr Hamblin to pay this time.

The *Gazette* had gained much-needed publicity the previous year, when it was just beginning daily publication. Blondin had been of great interest then. Now, the *Gazette* was no longer enthusiastic.

Neither were the railway company. The tailing off of ticket sales and even a number of empty seats on the later excursion trains made them reluctant to give their co-operation.

Everything seemed to go wrong with the first performance on 6 June 1860. The time set was four o'clock but at that time he could not find his balancing pole. It was over an hour before he could obtain another.

Less than 2,000 people turned up, and many of those left before he finally appeared on the rope at twenty past five. It was a routine crossing with one or two tricks, but the whole thing was over in seven minutes. The return was even shorter in five minutes.

Harry was in favour of 'cutting the losses' even at that late stage but Blondin announced he was 'building up to something special'. These were just preliminaries.

Two weeks later it was the same poor attendance. Only 300 people paid 25 cents to go into the enclosure which he had built at considerable cost on the American side. He had to contend with competition from the other side where only 3 cents was being charged by what the *Gazette* described as 'dilapidated people of both genders'. The railway company didn't do too well either; only about 500 people were on the bridge. More than 1,200 people watched it free. The head stand, which had made everybody gasp when first performed, rated only a murmur. The sack crossing drew a number of ribald comments and cries of 'Quack Quack' because of the waddling resemblance to a duck.

Again with hindsight, it is clear that attempting to repeat the events the following year was an act of folly. White thought so and would have nothing to do with the idea. Harry Colcord pointed to the diminishing returns at the end of the previous season and advised against an encore. Blondin would heed none of this guidance. Whether it was his unworldly, almost child-like innocence, or his need of applause, he would not believe that as a public attraction the thing was dead. Prodigious feats quickly become commonplace and, if anything, he had made them appear too easy.

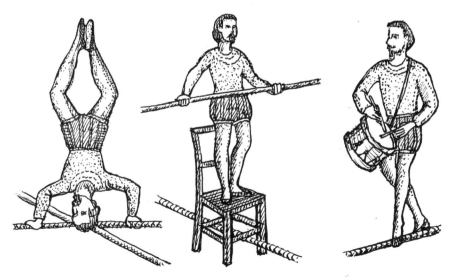

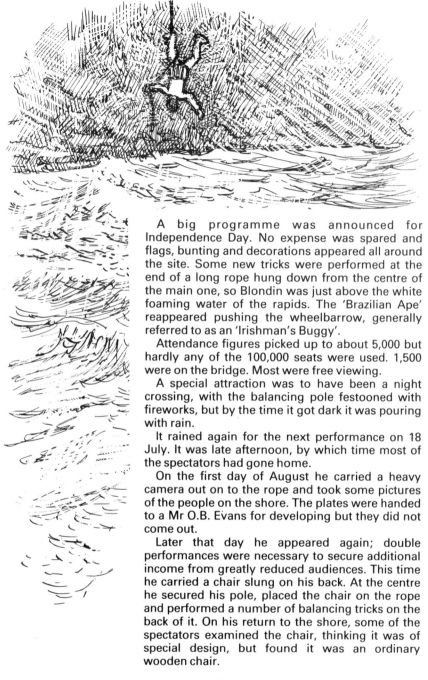

A big programme was announced for Independence Day. No expense was spared and flags, bunting and decorations appeared all around the site. Some new tricks were performed at the end of a long rope hung down from the centre of the main one, so Blondin was just above the white foaming water of the rapids. The 'Brazilian Ape' reappeared pushing the wheelbarrow, generally referred to as an 'Irishman's Buggy'.

Attendance figures picked up to about 5,000 but hardly any of the 100,000 seats were used. 1,500 were on the bridge. Most were free viewing.

A special attraction was to have been a night crossing, with the balancing pole festooned with fireworks, but by the time it got dark it was pouring with rain.

It rained again for the next performance on 18 July. It was late afternoon, by which time most of the spectators had gone home.

On the first day of August he carried a heavy camera out on to the rope and took some pictures of the people on the shore. The plates were handed to a Mr O.B. Evans for developing but they did not come out.

Later that day he appeared again; double performances were necessary to secure additional income from greatly reduced audiences. This time he carried a chair slung on his back. At the centre he secured his pole, placed the chair on the rope and performed a number of balancing tricks on the back of it. On his return to the shore, some of the spectators examined the chair, thinking it was of special design, but found it was an ordinary wooden chair.

On 11 August there was some shattering news. A Signor Farini, whose real name was William Leonard Hunt, had set up a rope on almost exactly the same position that Blondin had vacated. Farini announced that on the 15th he would 'eclipse all Blondin's performances'. The *Lockport Journal & Courier* was 'out Gazetting' the *Gazette* in its support of the new contender. The *Gazette* itself gave him more coverage than it was giving Blondin.

The new competitor quickly demonstrated that he was a very experienced and capable performer. He deliberately slackened the tension on his rope, so that it swayed alarmingly and made it appear much more difficult. Instead of raising a bottle from the deck of the *Maid of the Mist,* Farini lowered himself, head first, down to the deck and took a drink from a member of the crew. He duplicated all Blondin's tricks, with some additional refinements. Carrying a man across was not a problem, he stated, and he would soon do so.

There was little point in Blondin setting up a performance for the 15th, when Farini was to make his much publicised appearance. People would not walk all the way to the rapids when there was a new attraction much nearer. It would be too embarrassing if Blondin put on a show at the same time and lost out to the newcomer.

He decided to take up an offer to appear at Jones's Wood, New York. This was an open area of parkland close to the city centre, on the bank of the Hudson River. The rope was stretched from a tall pole in the woods out to an island off shore. It was a distance of about a quarter of a mile and the height was 200 feet (60.6m) above the river. Wind was the real hazard on this location. Blondin was paid a fee and did not have to rely on takings.

Returning to his hotel one evening, Blondin found a letter waiting. There was a crest on the envelope, and another on the letterheading. It was signed 'Comte A' and was from the young man whose life Blondin had saved when he fell overboard from the steamer nine years before. The letter was an invitation to join the Comte and a number of friends for dinner at his hotel. The greeting was warm and the Comte introduced Blondin as 'the second author of my life'. During dinner the young aristocrat urged Blondin to give up his dangerous profession; he would gladly pay all expenses back to France and use his influence with Emperor Napoleon III to secure a state appointment or some other means of permanently ensuring the future. The offer was declined with thanks, Blondin stating that he took no risks and pursued his profession from an inherent fondness for the art. At the end of the evening the Comte presented Blondin with a magnificent diamond ring.

For a time Blondin was fêted by the New Yorkers. Songs were composed in his honour. The appreciation of the crowd contrasted with the seemingly fickle indifference he was experiencing at Niagara. He wondered whether to cut his losses and remain where he was.

The proprietors of Jones's Wood gave him a pleasant surprise also. On one of his crossings at Niagara, he had been wearing the gold medal presented to him at the end of the previous season. It came loose somehow and fell into the river. A duplicate had been made and was now presented to him.

Royalty persuaded Blondin to return to Niagara. Edward, Prince of Wales and heir to the British throne, was visiting Niagara Falls and expressed a wish to see Blondin perform his crossing there. Since his boyhood days, and the appearance before the King of Sardinia, his respect for royalty had been absolute and there was not the remotest possibility of him not complying with the Prince's request. The appearance was fixed for 18 September.

There was time for another 'walk' by way of rehearsal and that took place on 29 August. Harry Colcord was carried across again, in spite of having vowed never to allow himself to be talked into it after the first time. It was easier on the second occasion; only two rests were required and the whole thing was completed in fifteen minutes.

Back at the original site, Farini chose this same day to duplicate Blondin's master achievement by carrying a man, named Rowland McMillen, across on his back, but by this time neither he nor Blondin was drawing big crowds.

On Saturday 18 September 1860, the 'Royal Command' performance took place. Edward, Prince of Wales, was the second child and eldest son of Queen Victoria and Prince Albert. At eighteen years of age he was very slim, good looking and charming. On this, his first official visit to America and Canada, he was already demonstrating his skill at diplomacy and winning admiration from all sides. He and his party arrived at the rapids on horseback about four o'clock.

Blondin was presented to the Prince and they chatted for a while, during which an offer was made to carry his Royal Highness across on the rope. To the consternation of his advisers, the Prince appeared to be seriously considering acceptance of the offer. The Duke of Newcastle, the Earl of St Germain, the Marquis of Chandos and Lord Lyons all joined in an anxious flurry of dissuasion, supported by the military aides General Williams, Major Teasdale and Major-General Bruce.

The performance commenced and the programme included all the tricks he had previously performed, leading up to Harry Colcord's third trip as passenger. At the end of the journey he too was presented. Both were given a purse containing 100 dollars. Harry was laughingly told that his was given on condition he never ever allowed himself to be carried across again. He never did.

Blondin then announced the special event he had been saving for this occasion. He would do the journey on stilts. The Prince urged him not to do it on his account but Blondin assured him there was no risk.

Blondin carried out the feat with the same apparent ease which he had always displayed. When he arrived safely, the Prince shook his hand and said 'Thank God it's over!'

Neither Farini nor anybody else equalled this performance at Niagara.

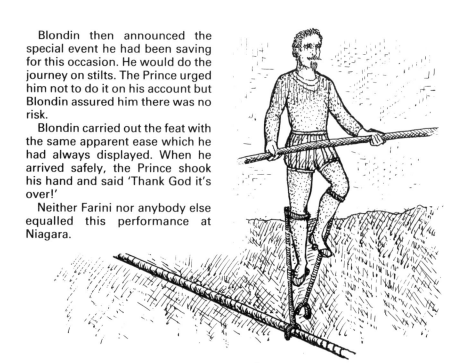

Harry Colcord decided he'd had enough of show business. With his 100 dollars and share of the takings, he used his undoubted ability as a portrait painter, aided by the publicity gained from his Niagara exploits, and spent the rest of his life as an artist.

Blondin thought of returning to his native France but there were many restrictions on his kind of activity there, and he abandoned the idea. One day, while visiting Gabriel Ravel at Niblo's Gardens, where the troupe was still appearing, Blondin was introduced to Henry Coleman. He was a dramatic author of international reputation, impresario and a theatrical manager with worldwide connections. Gabriel suggested that he should become Blondin's agent and a contract was signed at dinner the same evening.

Coleman recommended England and lost no time in sailing there on the German Lloyd liner *New York*, arriving at Southampton on the first day of May. He quickly set up a meeting with Mr George Grove, secretary of the Crystal Palace Company, and Mr R.K. Bowley, the manager. They introduced him to the Board of Directors. A proposal for a series of performances at the Palace was outlined, which was immediately accepted by all but one of the directors. 'But suppose he was to fall?' he enquired. 'To do what?' asked Coleman. 'Fall . . .' repeated the questioner. 'Fall!' said Coleman in an incredulous manner. 'Where from?' 'Why . . . from the rope'. 'Blondin! Fall from a rope! He can't'. The calm solemnity of this last reply completely demolished the solitary objection. A contract was drawn up for twelve appearances at a fee of £1,200. Four times more than the fee paid to any other performer.

There was great controversy about the Crystal Palace being used as 'a circus'. It was the brainchild of Prince Albert, and was built by Paxton as the centre piece for the Great Exhibition of 1851. It was subsequently transferred, at great expense, to Sydenham as a showcase for all that was best in British art and industry. It soon became apparent to the Board that there were insufficient people interested in such lofty ideals to make the place pay and the prospect of more commercial activity had great appeal.

Blondin's opening performance at Crystal Palace was on the first day of June 1861. Even at half-a-crown (2s.6d. – 12½p), plus another half-a-crown for a hard wooden seat, the Palace was filled to capacity and many were turned away.

The 'carriage trade' paid half a guinea (52½p) for a reserved seat on the Handel Orchestra platform of the uppermost gallery. The floor of the transept was kept clear for some yards on either side of the line of the rope – just in case.

Blondin had fixed his Niagara rope across the central transept, a distance of over 320 feet (96.9m) at a height of 170 feet (51.8m) above the floor. It was secured to a spiral staircase at each end. Weights were evenly distributed along the length of the rope to keep it taut and the guy ropes tied to the galleries on either side. The sag in the middle was 36 feet (10.9m). At either extremity a small platform was built about 8 feet (2.4m) above the highest gallery. Flags were draped to add a splash of colour and give a focal attraction.

At four o'clock, Blondin's assistant appeared at the west end platform and waved a flag to announce that the show was about to commence. The band of the Coldstream Guards struck up with bright marching music and Blondin appeared. There was applause, but the majority remained in awed silence as the scale of the drop was truly realised by the sight of the tiny figure above them.

He performed his repertoire of tricks and it was all over in half an hour, for which he received £100.

One of the people who was not turned away by the 'House Full' notices was Charles Dickens. He had just finished writing *Great Expectations*, which was assured of success on the wave of acclaim following the publication of *A Tale of Two Cities*, at about the time Blondin was making his first crossing at Niagara.

Dickens did not approve of such performances. He was not there to enjoy or admire; he had come to skit and scoff. He wrote about it in his most severely satirical style, to leave no doubt of his contempt.

'Here are ten thousand of us whom the train has poured from its cellular throat, driving up the passage of Crystal Palace like so many black peas up a pea-shooter. We have all but one object − to see a man walk on (or perhaps fall from) a rope a hundred feet high. We may tear buns to pieces, joint fowls and devour vast ledges of sandwiches, but still the one object of all of us − bishops, lawyers, authors, fashionables − is to see a rope dancer venture his life for one hundred pounds the half hour. For this purpose the sharp one toothed instrument has bit today through so many tickets; for this, vats of pale ale have been emptied; for this, Regent Street and the Parks have contributed armies of languid Herculeses and pale-powdered Venuses. For this, paralytic old Lady Chickenliver has been dragged here in her Bath chair, and even old Lord Stiffney has hobbled from his club ...'

It soon became clear to which aspect of such spectacles he objected.

'Half London is here, eager for some dreadful accident ...

'Everybody seems afraid that Blondin will fall before they are able to take their seats ... The chiding voice, whosoever it may be, is drowned by the tramp of unreasoning and hurrying feet.'

Punch made satirical comment in the form of an imaginary discussion between Dr Samuel Johnson and his biographer Boswell. The latter had bought a ticket to see Blondin at the Crystal Palace. It was written in the style of Boswell with dialogue characteristic of the famous doctor.

The sentiments were those of the editor of *Punch,* and he, like Dickens, was convinced that it was the prospect of disaster and not the performer's skill that was the attraction. The words put into the doctor's mouth included:

'You are a humbug! You care nothing for the fellow's courage or skill, but you have a vulgar desire to go with the multitude, and perhaps a concealed hope that you may be present at a painful catastrophe.'

In the feature, Johnson ends up by going to the performance himself, but protesting that he is really only going because everybody else is.

R. Flemin Lowell wrote a song:

'Of all the sights in England now,
And I've looked everywhere,
There is not one, of any sort,
With Blondin can compare;
He is the marvel of his age —
That everyone admits —
So, fit it is that he should beat
All others into fits;'

The chorus went:

'The world counts seven wonders up,
An eighth I will install,
The Hero of Niagara,
And greatest of them all.'

There were six more verses and the chorus after each.

Facsimiles of his signature appeared in support of various funds and charities.

Word got around, without any basis of fact, that the Crystal Palace directors were willing to pay the sum of £100 to anybody who would emulate Harry Colcord and be carried across the rope on Blondin's back. The office at the Palace was inundated with letters from all over the country. Some were quite absurd. One, from a university man, asked that his life be insured for £5,000 and an annuity settled on his children in case he was killed. Another 'weary of existence' was eager to avail himself of the opportunity of 'shuffling off this mortal coil'. Another asked for the money to be paid one month in advance, so that he may have the chance to spend it before he died. One husband offered to pay Blondin a hundred pounds if he would 'carry his wife over, and five hundred if he could manage to let her slip halfway'. A prerequisite of a 'feather bed of gigantic dimensions' was included in one of the letters; a 'huge pair of wings' in another.

There was only one way to stop all this correspondence; that was for Blondin to carry over a man of his own choosing. The man he decided upon was Natale Cavarazoni, an Italian who had been working as an assistant. Even then there was no shortage of volunteers, particularly amongst young guards officers, anxious to prove their courage or impress girlfriends. A charge of £5 to any selected only served to increase demand.

The Crystal Palace Company cleared £10,000 profit out of the twelve performances and Blondin duly received his £1,200. He had to pay Coleman's commission out of that, and the not inconsiderable costs of putting up and taking down the rope. Another contract was set up but the performer's terms were the same. Blondin complained in later life that he was always let down by his agents.

On 10 September Blondin carried James Rogers across the rope at the Crystal Palace. Rogers was one of the most popular comics on the London Music Hall stage.

The newspapers commented that he 'played his part well but it is not probable that he was desirous of a long run'.

In the days when a family of four could subsist on nine shillings (45p) a week, young men were queueing to pay £5 to be carried across by Blondin.

One of these was a young naval officer, who died an admiral sixty six years later. It was thought to be appropriate to include in his obituary that he had been one of those carried.

70

The desire to attempt something different led Blondin to devise a new feature for one of the programmes in the second series at the Crystal Palace. He told nobody of his plans beforehand; so there was consternation when Blondin appeared on the rope pushing his famous wheelbarrow, inside which was his five-year-old daughter Adèle. Garlanded with flowers she scattered rose petals on the crowd so far below. The child seemed perfectly relaxed and happy, and said in later years that she enjoyed every minute of it. This was too much for public opinion to stand. It was one thing for him to risk his own life, Harry Colcord's or any number of young officers', but not a child of five. Madame Blondin watched from the top gallery, perfectly confident in her husband's capabilities and that her child was safe. The entire family was at a loss to understand the furore which followed. The press called it an outrage! There were demands for instant legislation. Many wanted prosecution. The Home Secretary, Sir George Cornwall Lewis, sent an express letter to the Directors of the Crystal Palace calling on them to take immediate action on the matter. Blondin and Coleman were sent for and notified, in no uncertain manner, that it must never happen again.

During 1861 Charlotte and Jean François had a second son. He was christened Henry Coleman Gravelet.

Coleman next arranged a tour of the major provincial cities. 90,000 people turned out to see the performance at the Botanical Gardens in Sheffield, 70,000 at the Aston Fête in Birmingham.

Two years later, on 20 July 1863, Aston was the place where 'the female Blondin' was killed by falling from a high rope whilst trying to imitate one of his performances. She had watched his first appearance at the Crystal Palace. Her name was Young, but until then she had used the stage name Madame Genevieve. Her father and grandfather were both acrobats and she had achieved some reputation as a tightrope walker. By arrangement with E.T. Smith, the manager of the Cremorne Gardens, Chelsea, she attempted to cross the Thames on a tightrope by Chelsea Bridge but did not succeed. Insufficient attention had been given to the stability of the rope and it swayed so much she was unable to proceed. A line was thrown out to her from the bridge and she ignominiously climbed down into a boat. She continued to risk her life, almost losing it later that year in a trick involving fire. Aston Park, the scene of one of Blondin's great English triumphs, was where Madame Genevieve made her final appearance.

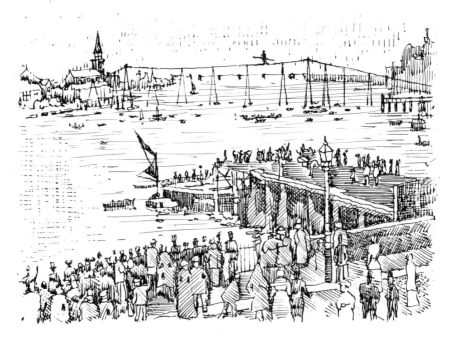

Wherever Blondin went, Manchester, Derby, Cheltenham, Dudley Castle ... he was a great success. At Belfast, he met an old friend who had fallen on hard times and provided the fare to send him to America, with money to give him a new start.

A return visit to Birmingham resulted in a near riot when a gang of sledgehammer roughs were refused entry to his performance. In the fighting which followed several constables were injured, four of them seriously; and the mounted police had to be called in to break up the disturbance. Seven of the ringleaders were later tried and received severe penalties.

At the Zoological Gardens in Liverpool, Blondin pushed a lion across the rope in his wheelbarrow. It proved to be more difficult than he had anticipated. The lion was named Tom Sayers, after the famous pugilist; it was strapped in the barrow and the journey began. The load was heavier than he had realised and his knees trembled with the exertion. To restrict the swaying, a guy rope was attached to the front of the barrow but this got tangled with the wheel some 50 feet (15.1m) out. The guy rope was jerked from the assistant's hands and there was a danger of tripping over it. Blondin decided to abandon the crossing and move back along to where he had started. There was complete silence as he edged his way cautiously. When he arrived, the guy was removed. Then, to everybody's surprise, he set out again. He reached the centre without any problem but then the uphill section began. It took enormous effort to make any progress at all. Several times the barrow slipped back again. It began to look as though it was going to prove too much for him. At last it was accomplished. He never attempted the feat again.

One of the autumn attractions at the Crystal Palace was the firework display in the grounds. It was decided that Blondin should participate by having his own display on an outdoor high rope set up over the fountains.

The Palace stood on high ground and one of the hazards at that time of year was fog descending very quickly. Even though a tightrope walker may operate blindfolded, fog tends somehow to affect the sense of balance and derange the nerves. Half-way through a performance fog suddenly came down and Blondin disappeared from view. For over thirty minutes anxious eyes searched upwards without seeing anything of him. Finally he reached the platform, having carried out the full programme, claiming that it did not upset him in the least.

On 31 October a more serious incident occurred. His act was to carry a load of fireworks out to the centre of the rope and discharge them there one at a time. Having done so, he proceeded to the other end where an assistant was waiting. It was necessary for the assistant to lift the grooved wheel off the rope and up on to the platform, because of the slight change of level. Blondin was standing holding the wheelbarrow's handles waiting to get off. The wheel was stuck for some reason and the assistant gave it a jerk to release it. This completely toppled Blondin off-balance. The pole, which was lying across the barrow, fell to the ground. Blondin saved himself by catching the rope with the back of his knee. It was a measure he had practised until it became instinctive and on this occasion it saved his life.

Madame Blondin was watching and this was the only time she was reported as 'having hysterics'.

A few days after this near disaster, the Blondins and Henry Coleman were invited to a sumptuous banquet in one of the rooms at the Crystal Palace, as guests of the Board of Directors. At the end of the meal Blondin was presented with another gold medal. It was the highest honour the board could bestow. The only other of its kind had been presented to Queen Victoria when she opened the Palace. The Frenchman was deeply moved and proudly wore the medal on every suitable occasion for the rest of his life.

74

1862 was even more successful than the previous year. There was a new contract to appear at the Crystal Palace; another for 200 performances in various London theatres amounting to £15,000. At £75 for each performance, this was a lower fee, but they were of shorter duration and at lower heights.

Blondin was now able to live in a manner befitting his success. He bought a house in the Finchley Road, St John's Wood, which he called Niagara Villa. There was a carriage and pair, with a groom to drive them about, servants and many other signs of prosperity.

The appearances at Crystal Palace were so popular that, on one occasion, Blondin was responsible for settling a trade dispute, although he was not aware of it at the time. The Annual Excursion of the London Cabmen's Friendly Society took place one Monday during the summer. It was an enjoyable event, but the cabmen had many grievances about conditions in their trade. At three o'clock a meeting was called under the chairmanship of Mr Maxwell. The leader of the Grievance Committee, Mr Llewellyn, wanted some militant action to demonstrate their solidarity. He seemed on the point of succeeding; then word got around that Blondin was about to appear on his rope. Within minutes the hall was empty – except for Mr Llewellyn!

Another time, Blondin was 'upstaged'. Thousands of people visited the Annual Monster Fête presented by the Ancient Order of Foresters, but feats on the tightrope were not as popular as an organised 'kissing' game, which seemed to be capable of being played by any number of couples, in any part of the grounds and at any time of the afternoon and evening.

In many ways 1862 was a momentous year.

England was still mourning the death of Prince Albert, which had occurred the previous December. The Crystal Palace, which had been inspired by him in 1851, was the centre of attention for a new Great Exhibition and Blondin was one of the attractions. He was introduced there to two rising politicians who attended one of his performances in each other's company – Mr Gladstone and Mr Disraeli.

In America, the Civil War was in its second year and Abraham Lincoln answered the critics of his government: 'Gentlemen, suppose all the property you were worth was in gold and you put it in the hands of Blondin to carry across the Niagara Falls on a rope. Would you shake the cable, or keep shouting out to him "Blondin! Stand up a little straighter; Blondin! Stoop a little more; go a little faster; lean a little more to the north; lean a little more to the south ...?" No you would hold your breath, as well as your tongue and keep your hands off until he was safely over!'

At the end of the season, a series of 'benefit' performances was organised at the Palace from which Blondin made a considerable amount of money.

At a reception, similar to that which he had given at Niagara, Blondin once again entertained the guests to a demonstration on the low tightrope, concluding with his carrying Madame Blondin across on his back. She was again reported as being 'very elegant'.

Henry Coleman decided it was time to move on. He did not want any repetition of the declining audiences that had happened at Niagara. A grand tour of Europe was arranged, which was scheduled to take the next two years.

As a farewell performance, Coleman wrote a special Christmas show. It was staged in the main central concourse of the Palace, where a large stage was built for the purpose. Mr Fenton, scenic artist of the Haymarket Theatre, painted the sets.

The show was described as a pantomimic drama and entitled *The Child of the Wreck*. It was merely a vehicle to demonstrate Blondin's climbing and acrobatic skills.

The action opened with a wreck scene in which Don Fernando, a Brazilian planter, witnessed the wreck of a vessel on which his wife and child were passengers. He succeeded in saving his wife but the child remained trapped on the wreck. It seemed certain she would be lost but she was rescued by a 'faithful ape', played by Blondin, who carried her off to a cave and took care of her. The mischievous animal drew attention to itself and was tracked back to its lair by a trapper called Sam. Seeing the child, Sam drew the wrong conclusion and shot the ape. Though dying, it thinks of 'its innocent charge' which it 'brings forth exultantly and restores to the astonished parents'. Then the ape dies 'as if satisfied with having done its duty'.

Adèle played the role of the child, and no exception was taken to this, even though some of the tricks were just as dangerous as crossing the rope. Blondin received great critical acclaim for his 'realistic portrayal'.

After a 'Farewell Performance' on the first day of February 1863, the Blondin family and Henry Coleman set off on the Grand Tour.

They went first to France where the major cities all staged performances, culminating in Paris. A proposal to cross the Seine from one of the towers of Notre Dame was firmly turned down by the authorities. In recognition of his achievements, the Emperor, Napoleon III, conferred on Blondin the rank of Chevalier of the Legion of Honour.

In Madrid he was appointed a Chevalier of the Order of Queen Isabel of Spain.

The Russian Tzar Nicholas received him and remarked that he was 'very little to be so great'. As a mark of royal favour he was given a diamond tie pin. The Grand Duke Constantine, who was present at the time, said it was a pity Blondin was not a soldier.

Portugal and Italy both received him as a hero and people turned out in their thousands to cheer him.

In 1864, they went to South America. His fame had not reached there. An agent said to Henry Coleman 'Blondin? Who is Blondin?' to which Henry replied 'You must have been in jail a long time!' It was symptomatic of the general reception, and the tour there was a 'dead loss'.

It was a gruelling two years and a huge success in terms of public acclaim, and flattering in the number of crowned heads by whom he was received.

The expenses were enormous and, while hundreds of thousands had cheered, a much smaller number had been willing to pay to see a performance. Once again it was a speculative venture, where returns depended on gate money.

There was fame but not a lot of cash!

Their daughter Charlotte was to be the Blondins' last and she was born in 1866.

For the great French Exposition of 1867 Blondin again offered to cross the Seine from Notre Dame, with all the proceeds going to charity. The authorities would only permit this if a net was used for safety, so the offer was withdrawn. He was probably correct in assuming that, with a net, there would be fewer watchers.

The Blondins had originally intended to return to America, Charlotte Sophia's birthplace. By the time the European tour was over, the American Civil War was at its height, so the decision was postponed. The troubled situation, following Lincoln's assassination, put off the decision again. They were nicely settled in St John's Wood and enjoyed a high standard of living, even if the hated income tax, imposed by the government, had never been taken off at the end of the Crimean War as promised. There was enough invested capital to enable him to retire and, as he was now forty years of age, he felt it was time to do so. For the next seven years, the family dropped out of the public view. The time was spent happily in a quiet life and much travel.

A long trip was arranged for the following year. It was to Australia and New Zealand. A small number of demonstrations had been arranged and the Niagara rope travelled with the luggage. They all embarked on the s.s. *Poona* for the first stage of the journey to India via the Suez Canal, which had opened four years before.

The *Poona* was one of the largest vessels in the Peninsular and Orient Line, measuring over 430 feet (130.3m) in length. Out in the Indian Ocean, Blondin decided to keep in practice by walking on a rope stretched between the two masts of the ship. The weather was calm and the Captain, not wishing to offend such a famous passenger, agreed, thinking it would also amuse the other voyagers. The Niagara rope was secured by guys to the rails along either side of the ship.

The ship was steaming at 12 knots. When Blondin was half-way across the rope a sudden tropical storm brought rain and huge waves. The alarmed passengers caught on deck watched, both horrified and fascinated, as Blondin fought against the rain before he finally made it to safety. He later described it as a nightmare and the most difficult performance in his life.

After their stay in India they moved on to Australia.

The ship for this stage of their journey was the s.s. *Flintshire.* Just outside Sydney harbour the ship ran on to a sandbank. The crew succeeded in winching her off by the anchors at high tide but there was considerable damage to the cargo. The Blondins lost all their luggage, and the precious Niagara rope, used as an exhibit, was damaged beyond repair.

Nobody had been injured and the ship limped into the harbour.

His appearances were just as popular in Australia as they were in New Zealand where he received a warm and congenial welcome.

Another medal was added to his collection to mark this trip. It was a cross of Australian gold on which were emblems of a Kangaroo and an Emu worked in precious stones. Another token he received, and was greatly amused by, was an anonymous note which read:

'A noad to mr Blondin: remarkable pusson! enterprisin' strainger! You probably started on a railwa trac, or praps a curb ston: then you took to fensis; and then you soured to rafters in noo houses. Remarkable pusson! By merely a taikin' ov a walk you clear 1,000 dolers nearly every time. Then the Hier you get the Straiter you kin walk, this shows you ain't at al like common foax, wich can't walk much when they are Elevated.'

The next year they travelled to South America again, and by now his reputation was well known there. He seemed to have hit on a happy formula; by making one or two selected appearances he could pay the entire expenses of the trip and travel first class. At one performance he carried the nine-year-old Charlotte on his back. He had previously done so on many occasions, using a lower rope, but had always secured her on to his back for safety. This time the act was performed on a high rope and he forgot to tie her on. She didn't mind a bit, but he was horrified and never carried her on a rope again.

In 1879 Blondin lost all his money.

Various reports gave differing causes: the *Niagara Falls Gazette* said it was 'a bank failure'. Another newspaper reported it as 'bad investment in the wine trade'. One paper stated 'an unscrupulous individual ran away with it'. Whatever the cause, the days of retirement were over. At fifty five years of age, he had to start working again.

Niagara Villa had to go, and was sold to 'Pony' Moore, a well known figure in racing and gambling circles. The carriage and pair went too, along with the servants. A semi-detached house of a more modest size was bought, No 6 Boscobel Gardens, near Marylebone Station.

A gambler bet £10,000 he would not reach his 60th birthday and is said to have attended every performance during the following five years.

Blondin had lost nothing of his old skill and within a year he had made many 'ascensions', including some at Brussels, Vienna and as far away as Ceylon (now Sri Lanka).

In 1882 he appeared on the site of the Alexandra Palace, in London. This had opened to the public seven years before but burned down within the year. Proposals were under discussion for a replacement building and meanwhile the park was kept open, and a programme of entertainment maintained. Blondin appeared there a number of times during the seasons which followed, and earned high fees.

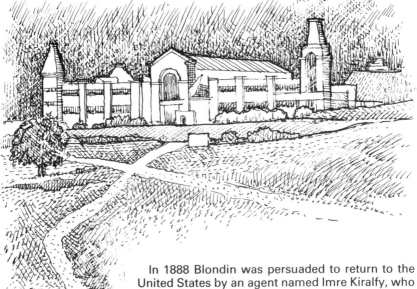

In 1888 Blondin was persuaded to return to the United States by an agent named Imre Kiralfy, who held out a promise of a venue in Central Park, New York. There was so much public protest about the appearance that permission was refused.

Blondin knew nothing of the ban until he arrived in New York on 4 June. Kiralfy attempted to explain the situation by saying: 'It's easier to get parks in foreign countries because monarchs can be controlled better than republics. There's only one to kick in a monarchy. Here, there are millions to kick!'

The only place where a site could be found was on Statten Island, dominated by the Immigrants' Reception Centre. It was not a happy alternative to Central Park. There were many things that were not to Blondin's liking. After only one week, he asked to be released from his contract and this was agreed. He returned to England by the first available boat, but it had been a dismal and costly failure.

In any case it was not a happy sixty fifth year but, at the end of it, his wife died.

Charlotte Sophia Gravelet was buried at Kensal Green Cemetery, London, on 19 December 1888.

The family had all left home: Adèle had married Frank Pastor, an American circus rider and brother of Tony Pastor the famous impresario but was already widowed and living in South London. Edward, the elder son, was of a roving disposition and they had lost touch with him years before. Iris was now Mrs D'Anguilar and lived in South America. Henry was married and lived in Brentford. Charlotte was Mrs Robbiolo.

Blondin at sixty five was a favourite figure for the cartoonist. The controversies surrounding his appearances often brought about unflattering remarks.

The following year Blondin had Niagara House built on a plot of land in Northfield Lane, Little Ealing.

When not making frequent appearances on the tightrope at various venues throughout the country, he was breeding dogs, raising chickens and spending many hours making things. He was a skilled craftsman and years before had redesigned an ice skate after his wife had injured her ankle while skating in New York, using the conventional model of the day. The modifications he introduced greatly improved the performance of the skate and his ideas were incorporated as standard design.

Blondin never practised new tricks. Even the most difficult were carefully worked out in his mind before their first performance but never actually rehearsed. Once done, he could repeat them at any time. This allowed him to give great variety in his work and his programme never became monotonous. After a year or more, without setting foot on a rope, he could step out and do his act as though in constant practice. When walking on the rope he looked about twenty feet ahead and whistled or hummed snatches of tunes to himself. If there was a band he kept in step with the rhythm.

A new prop was introduced into the act; the velocipede. Built on similar lines to the famous wheelbarrow, it had grooved wheels to fit the rope and a low centre of gravity. It became a popular feature in his appearances and was later copied by many other rope walkers. As far as can be ascertained, he was the first to use a bicycle in this way.

During the 1960s, both the velocipede and the wheelbarrow were found in a London junk shop by Blondin's grandson. They were subsequently bought and taken to Niagara Falls.

By the 1880s a sector of the press was calling for the outright banning of all life-risking perform-ances. There was some justification for this and a large measure of support – it is no longer permiss-ible to go over Niagara Falls in a barrel. But the criteria for deciding what is, or is not, life-risking are not clear. Acrobats had been killed falling off ropes a few feet above the floor. Blondin pointed out that, in many cases, the practical aspects may become easier and gave as an instance that his rope, to span the Niagara Gorge, had to be so thick that the young apprentice at the beginning of his training would have found no difficulty in walking it.

Controversy intensified during his career, but it was as old as entertainment, and will continue as long as there are people.

The Examiner summed up the anti-feelings in a leader entitled 'The Bad Eminence' which began by describing Blondin as 'The Mountebank at the Crystal Palace' who was, it said, 'praised for his foolhardiness in making moderate skill as a tightrope walker "attractive" by performing his tricks at peril of his life instead of limb'.

Blondin had no illusions about this. He constantly said that this was a major factor, probably 'the factor,' which attracted the crowds.

Walter Pelham's *Illustrated Journal* almost returned to the medieval beliefs that acrobats were in league with the Devil, portraying him in evening dress in the box eagerly awaiting a heretic soul.

The Crystal Palace directors yielded to pressure and insisted that Blondin should use a safety net. He pointed out that he had no experience of falling into nets from a great height, and was quite likely to break his neck doing so. They would not relent, and neither would he, so for a time there were not any appearances there.

When he was seventy years old the Board were particularly keen to have him back, so a compromise was offered. They would agree to do away with the net, provided the rope was lowered to 60 feet (18.2m). He refrained from pointing out the obvious and accepted the compromise. He did not intend to fall off any rope, irrespective of its height.

He appeared there on Boxing Day, thirty three years after his first visit. He had been performing for sixty five years and estimated he had made some 4,000 'ascensions'.

Shortly after that, there was an occasion when a net would have been most useful. It was while he was appearing at the Paragon Theatre. While carrying a chair during a trick, it fell but was caught and nobody was hurt. The papers commented: 'Chairs may come and chairs may go, but Blondin goes on for ever'.

While appearing at Blackpool in 1895, Blondin strained his back during a performance. He tried to continue, though in severe pain, but it was impossible and there were fears he would fall. Barely able to stand, he was taken by cab to his hotel. The doctors ordered total rest and constant nursing.

Katherine James was in charge and, as the Middlesex County News reported, 'not for the first time in history, a patient fell in love with his nurse!' She was thirty — not twenty seven as reported — he seventy one, but the affection was mutual. They married two months later, in the Brentford Registry Office. There was no time for a honeymoon because the next day he travelled to Glasgow, where he had a two week booking.

Mr and Mrs Gravelet continued to live quietly at Niagara House and added horses to the menagerie of dogs and chickens. People who passed by often got a wave from the famous man — or even a somersault.

Jean François Gravelet who, as Blondin, had taken such appalling risks with his life, died in his bed peacefully, at seventy three. The cause of death was diabetes.

He was buried, in Kensal Green Cemetery, on 19 February 1897. His estate was valued at £2,500, about the same as he had earned for six half hour appearances at Crystal Palace. The money, and a portrait of his first wife, were left to Katherine. She was not to survive him long, but died in 1901 of cancer, at the age of thirty six.

In his time, Blondin was given many impromptu titles: 'The Little Wonder'; 'Emperor of Manila'; 'Lord of the Hempen Realm'; 'Hero of Niagara'. He was jokingly called 'the most conceited man in the world' because 'he looked down on everyone'. Another label he would not have liked was 'first of the Niagara stunters'.

He would have abhorred the word 'stunter' because he believed stunts, though courageous, were not a test of ability. When Sam Patch leapt from his platform he was bound to hit the water; Annie Taylor became the first person to go over Horseshoe Falls in a barrel on 4 October 1901. Probably, Blondin would have said: 'If a barrel is put in the rapids above the Falls, it will go over them. If somebody is inside the barrel that person will go over too.'

Even though Blondin's original vision to bridge the Horseshoe Falls on a strand of rope was not realised, he had demonstrated to the world that he was not a stunter but an artist who had passed his own 'test of ability' with distinction.

93

ACKNOWLEDGEMENTS

THE BRITISH LIBRARY

THE NEWSPAPER LIBRARY

OTHER BRITISH LIBRARIES:

Aberdeen
Birmingham
Brentford
Bromley
Chiswick
Ealing
Hounslow
Liverpool
Manchester
Westminster

OTHER LIBRARIES:

Niagara Falls
Ontario
Buffalo
Rochester
Earl Bridges, New York
French Institute
French Embassy

OTHER SOURCES:

V & A Theatre Museum
Public Records Office
Census Office
Registrar General
Kelly's Directory
Middlesex Directory
Electoral Rolls
Rate books
Crystal Palace Foundation
Alan Warwick papers
Registers of Kensal Green Cemetery
Annual Registers

NEWSPAPERS & MAGAZINES

The Times
Illustrated London News
Pelham's Weekly
Punch
Middlesex Times
Daily Mail
Niagara Falls Gazette
St Catherine's Journal
Buffalo Morning Express
Buffalo Daily Courier
New York Daily Gazette
Daily Spectator
Lockport Journal and Courier
Buffalo Post
Lockport Advertiser
Daily Globe
St Louis Sunday Republican
New York Daily Tribune
Lockport Chronicle
Albany Evening Chronicle

Boston Advertiser
Niagara Falls Review
The Graphic

ARTICLES:

'Blondin, the hero of Niagara'
Lloyd Graham, 1950
American Heritage

'Falls mark Blondin Day'
1948
Niagara Falls Gazette

'Niagara River, Feats and Tragedies'
1936
Edward T. Williams
Federal Writer's Project

'Niagara, scene of perilous feats'
Orin E. Dunlap, 1902
Cosmopolitan

OTHER WORKS:

'Niagara Daredevils'
Willis E. Beese, 1949
Renown

'Blondin March'
Albert Poppenberg

'Niagara'
Greenhill and Mahoney, 1969
University of Toronto Press

'Hero of Niagara'
By one who has known him all his
    life, 1873
Free Press

'Niagara Falls and Blondin'
J. Sage, 1861

'The Early Doors'
Harold Scott, 1977
E.P. Publishing

'Blondin, his life and
    performances'
G. Linnaeus Banks, 1862
Routledge, Warner and Routledge

'Niagara and the Daredevils'
Philip Mason, 1969
Daredevils' Gallery

'Daredevils of Niagara'
Andy O' Brian
The Ryerson Press, Toronto

'Blondin, Hero of Niagara'
Richard A. Boning
Dexter & Westbrook, N.Y.

'The Niagara River'
Archer Butler Herbert, 1908
G.P. Putnam's Sons, N.Y.

'Anthology and Bibliography of
    Niagara Falls'
Charles Mason Dow, L1D, 1921
State of New York